A MARRIAGE GOD'S WAY

Till Death DO US PART

JACKIE CALLOWAY

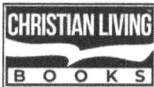

CHRISTIAN LIVING
B O O K S

Largo, MD

Christian Living Books, Inc.
christianlivingbooks.com
We bring your dreams to fruition.

ISBN 9781562295875

DEDICATION

I dedicate this book to Mrs. Stacy Bond Davis and Mrs. Lynette Gilbert, the two head registered nurses who gave Ronnie the very best care possible. You ladies went far above and beyond your call of duty. All of your tender loving care was done from your hearts. That was so obvious to me. Ronnie ministered to you until he couldn't as you continuously ministered to him. Both of you taught me how to be an unregistered nurse to my husband. As you know, you are now official members of our Calloway family.

To the other nurses who were assigned to Ronnie's case, especially Fasil, Toni and Lucia; my heartfelt thanks to you. You were all like angels on assignment. I will forever be grateful to Trusted Ally Home Health Care, you are the best in my *book*, no pun intended.

To my editor Mrs. Lauren W. Willis, Thank you thank you thank you!

TABLE OF CONTENTS

PREFACE

I have written this book at the urging of the Holy Spirit. His prompting is for me to share with the world what a marriage God's way looks like. That is the purpose of this writing. In this book you will learn how God reconciled Ronnie Calloway and myself after seven years of divorce first to Himself and then to one another. To the best of our ability, we followed His instructions. God desires that all married couples experience a love that will not let you go. Love from Him and love from your spouse. You can have love and peace like you never dreamed possible. All God needs are two willing and yielded disciples to obey Him. Follow God's instructions and receive God's results. The benefits are miraculous and so much fun.

CHAPTER 1

A MARRIAGE GOD'S WAY

No, no, no, God I won't listen to Ronnie Calloway. You know he's a liar You know I can't trust him!! God said to me, "I'm *not* asking you to trust him right now, I'm asking you to trust Me with all of your heart, and lean not to your own understanding. In all your ways acknowledge Me and I will direct your paths." (Proverbs 3:1-6 AMP) I was furious!!

That was my response to God before He miraculously reconciled Ronnie and myself, first to Himself and then to one another. This reconciliation and restoration came after seven years of an ugly divorce. My goal in writing this book is not to dwell on the gory details of the previous marriage and the divorce; on the contrary, my heartfelt desire is to give you a glimpse of the beautiful twenty-four-year marriage God gave to us after we finally obeyed Him. God always has a plan and a purpose for everything He does and asks us to do. Sadly, sometimes we miss His plan as I almost did.

God said to me, "I want you to listen to Ronnie Cal-loway." When I heard that, I was furious. I certainly did not want to do that. God didn't tell me to marry him, just to listen to him; so, I reluctantly obeyed. I didn't realize that Ronnie had prayed and asked God to give him back his family. That made no difference to me because I didn't want him back.* Please find details of this in my first book *Love That Would Not Let Me Go.*

Once I realized what God was trying to do through us, I started to pay attention. He said to me, "I will restore to you the years the locust has eaten-the hopping locust, the stripping locust, and the crawling locust, My great army which I sent among you. And you shall eat in plenty and be satisfied and praise the name of the Lord, your God, Who has dealt wondrously with you. And My people shall never be put to shame." (Joel 2:25-26) I still didn't want

---

* Again, I refer you to my previous book *Love That Would Not Let Me Go* for all of those details.

to deal with Ronnie Calloway again. However, I thought, maybe that meant God will give me a house as a part of that restoration. The last house we owned in Georgia was repossessed.

One day after praying and then being quiet, the Lord told me, "I will restore to you the *quality* of the years you lost in your former marriage." The *quality* of years? I didn't know what that meant yet, I reluctantly obeyed God as only He knew I would.

Keep in mind God didn't tell me to marry Ronnie right then; He instructed me just to listen to Him. As I listened to Ronnie consistently day after day, I heard a new man. Please don't think I just fell into Ronnie's arms and we started all over again. No, I sent him through a rigorous inquisition. I questioned him about all of his prior devilish lifestyle. To my knowledge he was honest with me. He admitted to me everything I asked and volunteered even more than I asked.

After my listening to Ronnie and his wooing me for approximately three months, he proposed. In February 1996, Ronnie got down on one knee and asked me to marry him. I said, "Yes." By that time, I had actually started having fun with him. It was difficult for me to believe that I had come to this place of forgiveness and reconciliation. It was only through prayer and the grace of God that this was happening. We prayed a lot. I thought about Luther Vandross singing, I DON'T WANT TO BE A FOOL ANYMORE. I couldn't survive another heart break.

Over the months, Ronnie had thoroughly convinced me that it would be to my advantage to be his wife again. He pleaded with me to give him a chance to make it up to me for all the pain and heartache he had caused me previously. He was so sincere.

We had not set a wedding date yet, but we both agreed that we should have pre-marital counseling. Eagerly we did that. Ronnie and I also agreed that we would bury all of the past hurts, never to dig any of that up again. Miraculously we did that also. Again, that was possible only by the grace of God. He asked me to listen to Ronnie Calloway and to trust Him with all of my heart. He is so Faithful!

In March 1996, Ronnie came to me again, got down on one knee, took my hand and said, "Jackie Smith Calloway, I love you with all of my heart. I know I have hurt you in the past; but, I want to make all of that up to you. If you marry me, you will never have to work another day in your life." He choked and grabbed his throat when he said that. "I want to spend the rest of my life taking care of you and making you happy. Will you marry me?"

He put a beautiful, three-karat, diamond ring on my finger, and I said, "Yes, I will marry you Ronnie Calloway."

On April 19, 1996 we were married at Scott United Methodist Church. This was not a remarriage it was a *new* marriage. Nevertheless, God wanted to continue the lineage of our family. God made our family whole again. There were almost three hundred people at our wedding. WOW, what a wedding.* God likes weddings. Jesus' first miracle was performed at a wedding. (John 2:1-12 KJV) Our reconciliation was another miracle He performed at our wedding.

CHAPTER 2

A MIRACLE AND FIREWORKS ON OUR HONEYMOON

Our wedding night and honeymoon were epic. I'm sure most couples could say the same about their honeymoon. Nonetheless, this was unique for both of us. We were two mature people who knew each other very well, but didn't really know one another at all. We had been divorced for seven years. I was fifty years young and Ronnie was fifty-two. Many changes had taken place in both of us over the seven years. I had become stronger emotionally. I had learned I could depend on Jesus Christ to supply all of my need according to His riches in glory by Christ Jesus. (Philippians 4:19) Ronnie had developed a more intimate relationship with Jesus Christ during his year of homelessness. He was definitely not the same Ronnie I had divorced. Both of us were seven years older and hopefully more mature. We were feeling our way through.

Our middle daughter Rhonda worked for Marriott hotels at that time. When she asked for time off to attend our wedding, her boss thought ours was such a Cinderella story that he wanted to participate. He gave us five days at the Marriott hotel in San Diego, California overlooking Coronado Island for $39.00 per night. It normally would have been much more expensive than that. That gift was the favor of God to us.

After the wedding reception we retreated to our Marriott hotel in Denver near the Airport. We were both exhausted after all of the festivities and the week of preparation for the wedding.

We laid down and rested for a little while looking at the ceiling. We laughed and talked about everything that had happened.

Ronnie asked, "Can you believe all of the people that showed up to our wedding?"

"I was just as surprised as you were," I replied. "This wedding truly exceeded our expectations."

After resting and talking awhile, we turned to each other. Our counselor had advised us to pray in the Spirit before we made love. We did that and the love making was the very best it had ever, ever been in all of our previous twenty-eight years of marriage. Ronnie said it was like the Fourth of July and New Years' Eve combined. God blessed us in such a way that we wept tears of joy to be reunited. It was truly supernatural. It is difficult to put into words. We enjoyed such a tender, sweet, and peaceful night as we held each other close until morning.

The next morning, we awakened, packed our bags and proceeded to the airport, and boarded the plane for San Diego, California for a fun-filled honeymoon week. We were like two teenagers getting to know each other again. We felt very comfortable and safe with one another.

Ronnie said to me several times, "I missed you so much."

I replied, "I missed you too love." We were reunited and it felt so good.

Ronnie said, "Jack, let's live!" We don't have any kids to be concerned about anymore, let's live our lives like we want to live."

I said to him, "Hey, I'm in agreement with you brotha, let's do it." And we did for the next twenty-four wonderful joy filled God blessed years; we lived.

The favor of God was all over us. One night on our honeymoon we planned to go to dinner at this nice restaurant on the water in San Diego. When we arrived the manager said, "I'm sorry sir we just closed."

"Oh no you can't be closed Ronnie replied; this is our honeymoon. We've been in bed all day and we need some nourishment."

The manager laughed and said, "Okay come on in and we'll make you dinner." We were delighted. We were the only ones in the restaurant and they treated us royally. God is so good.

CHAPTER 3

GOD'S PLAN AND PURPOSE

One of the reasons God reconciled Ronnie and me was to manifest, and make known to the world His purpose for marriage. God allowed us to model marriage God's way. Of course, we didn't realize that at first. God was giving both of us instructions individually and collectively as we went along. We learned that we both had to have an intimate relationship with Jesus Christ. We spent time in the Bible and in prayer by ourselves every day, and I do mean every day. Most days we came together and compared notes.

A question we frequently asked one another was, "What is the Holy Spirit saying to you today?" Then we took turns sharing what was on our hearts. Not surprisingly to us, it would usually be something concerning how we should conduct ourselves in this marriage.

I would never say our marriage was perfect, it *was not*. We are flawed individuals. However, God kept both of us in line with His Word. When we said or did the wrong thing, we would come aside with Him. Those were His instructions to me before we married. "Don't argue with Ronnie. If you don't agree, just come aside to Me and pray. I will direct your paths." Proverbs chapter three was always front and center in my mind.

You may ask what does come aside with Me look like? Often, I went into my prayer room to tell God on Ronnie about something he may have said that I didn't agree with. God usually checked me about my attitude. Are you doing the Word Jackie? As I started to apologize to Ronnie, but Ronnie pulled me to himself, kissed me passionately, and apologized to me. In twenty-four years, we never let the sun go down on our wrath. (Ephesians 4:26) That in itself was supernatural to me. We did not go to bed angry at one another in twenty-four years.

CHAPTER 4

$\mathcal{R}$ECONCILED FOR GOD'S PURPOSE

$\mathcal{T}$he word reconcile as defined in Webster's dictionary means to make friendly again or to win over to a friendly attitude. 2) to settle a quarrel, difference. 3) to make arguments, ideas, texts accounts etc. consistent, compatible, etc.; bring into harmony 4) to make content submissive, or acquiescent.

Our reconciliation was quite different. Our reconciliation was a divine supernatural reconciliation that only God could have made happen.

From the beginning, I was totally opposed to this reunion. However, three months prior to Ronnie's asking me to come back to him, the Holy Spirit had impressed upon me to meditate on the Scripture passage in Proverbs.

The particular version of the Bible that I meditated on and visualized for approximately three months was the Amplified Bible. It reads:

> Lean on, trust in, and be confident in the Lord with *all* your heart and mind and do not rely on your own insight or understanding. In *all* your ways know recognize, and acknowledge Him, and He will direct and make straight and plain your paths. Be not wise in your own eyes, reverently fear and worship the Lord and turn entirely away from evil. It shall be health to your nerves and sinews and marrow and moistening to your bones. (Proverbs 3:5-8 AMP)

For three months I read, reread, memorized and visualized that passage of scripture over and over again. I had memorized every word of significance, defined and meditated on them. Muttered them over and over. I actually, thought about them day and night. I knew the Lord was preparing me for something, but I had no idea it would be this marriage.

One section of verse seven says to turn entirely away from evil. To me that meant to turn entirely away from anything contrary to God's Word. For instance, unforgiveness, talking about and judging people, and certainly unbelief.

I had forgiven Ronnie but at first, I sure did not want to believe that God wanted me to go back to him. Nonetheless, verse five says do not rely on your own insight or understanding. My own insight and understanding were that this brotha had been unfaithful to me for years and my understanding was that he could be unfaithful and hurt me again. However, the Holy Spirit had convinced me not to rely on that. Then verse eight says be not wise in your own eyes.

What is significant about me having the courage to listen to Ronnie again is:

God said to me, "I want you to listen to Ronnie Calloway, but trust Me with all your heart." That was the conundrum for me. How do I listen to Ronnie while at the same time trust God with all of my heart? That sounded like an oxymoron to me.

I was a little afraid but mostly angry at first. I thought this was very unfair to me. The very idea of God wanting me to open my heart again to even listen to him didn't seem right. But, I have always known God to be more than fair and certainly just with me. It was a process but I trusted Him. I had learned to trust God as a teenager.**

I've always known Him to be true to His word. There were times when Ronnie was talking, but I would shift my focus to Jesus; while looking in Ronnie's eyes. I would say to myself, "God I'm trusting you not this boy." As it turned out God was more than fair to both of us.

It was the love of God that would not let me go. That is one reason I knew I could trust Him in this marriage.

God's reconciliation is different from the dictionary's definition of that word. God doesn't restore things or people to their original state. Ronnie and I learned that our heavenly Father does exceedingly abundantly above all we could ask or think according to the power that works in us. (Ephesians 3:20 KJV) That is what He did with us.

Ronnie's transformation was amazing. At first it was difficult for me to believe. He told me that God had met him nose to nose when we were divorced. Ronnie was homeless living in a utility van that didn't run for almost a year through the winter months in Colorado. The Lord told him, "You can't live without Me!" He said he didn't know exactly what that meant. Sounded clear to me.

After God healed him from a disease he had contracted, he went back to church and got permanently serious with God. Ronnie learned obedience through what he had suffered.

Ronnie's love for me in this new marriage was stronger and more sincere than I had ever seen or felt before. He allowed God to love me through Him. He sincerely yielded to God the Father and committed to doing God's word and His will. He admitted to me that God gave him instructions in how to win me back.

I was very skeptical at first but as time went on there was nothing to be skeptical of. We were yielded to God and His word so our security was not in each other but in Him.

God had revealed Himself to us before we married. Our union was a three-fold cord that could not easily be broken. (Ecclesiastes 4:12 KJV) We realized we were reconciled and married for a purpose. The Holy Spirit gradually revealed that purpose to us. God chose to demonstrate what marriage His way looks like. That plan and purpose was cemented in our hearts over time.

Ronnie treated me like a precious diamond. He was careful to open every door, hold every chair as I sat. He always wanted to hold my hand or put his arm around me, and it was consistently the same at home, or in public. It didn't matter. He made me his queen. I returned his affection gracefully. That was easy to do. For a few months after the wedding, I waited for the other shoe to drop. Instead, ours became a deeper and more intense love for one another.

God's reconciliation is different, it doesn't compare to the world's definition at all. This marriage and both of us far exceeded what we thought we could do or ever become. We consistently followed Christ Jesus' instructions. We were experiencing, God loving us through each other.

My first instruction from God was to "Shut up. Just stop talking so much. Do more listening to Ronnie and to Me." I prayed the Word of God:

> Set a watch O LORD, before my mouth;
> keep the door of my lips. (Psalm 141:3)

He told me, "If you ever become angry with Ronnie and want to argue, just come aside with Me first. A few times I slipped, expressing my opinion, but I got better as time passed.

We became comfortable with each other while continuing to enjoy ourselves. We were wide open and yielded to how God was leading us. By now, our family was on board with us. My mother was very happy we were back together. Our girls and sons-in-law acted as if the divorce never happened. The grandchildren at that time were only three and one year old. As our family observed us, there were no objections from anyone any more.

CHAPTER 5

A PLEASANT PERSONALITY WORKS IN ONE'S FAVOR

Ronnie had several life-long friends. He was a very likeable and popular guy. Mr. *Smooth* some called him. I can't leave out the fact that he was cute also and he knew it. Ronnie never met a stranger. He usually had something to say to almost everybody about almost everything. The ladies certainly loved him. He made people feel special.

Ronnie loved his friends. He kept in touch with many of the friends he grew up with. They got together and talked about elementary and high school days. Ray Chapman, Elmer Tinsley, Dennis, Preston and Buba Doo. One of their favorite topics of conversation was to remember the fights they had with different people growing up. They sometimes couldn't remember why they fought; they just remembered the fight.

Every year Manual High School in northeast Denver, hosted a city-wide picnic. No matter where you went to school, everyone was invited to this event. Ronnie told people that this was his birthday party. His "invitation" only worked because the picnic always fell on the week of his birthday in August. Ronnie said to strangers he met, "I want to invite you to my birthday party. Bring your friends and all your family, and you can bring me a birthday present too." I thought that was so funny because that was so Ronnie Calloway. I loved that guy so much.

I only mention his relationship with his friends for one reason. They all noted the definite change in Ronnie after we were married and after He yielded his life to Jesus Christ. His nickname in high school was Candy Man. Now, he was God's man. Dennis Irvin was Ronnie's best friend from childhood. They talked on the phone for hours year after year.

Golf was Ronnie's main hobby, skill and passion. He was a scratch golfer and developed many life-long friendships over the years. Ronnie told the golfers they couldn't curse if they wanted to play with him. Several of his golf buddies were constantly striving to beat him on the course. Ronnie would tell them, "Stop trying to beat me, and try to beat the course."

One of Ronnie's golf buddies Jeffrey, told me that golfers talked about many different subjects while on the course. Jeffrey said, "Ronnie always talked about how much he loved his wife. He said, Ronnie talked about how much fun you and he had together and how thankful he was that you were together again." It was such a blessing for me to hear those words.

Ronnie was an RTD bus driver for twenty-one years. He was well known as one of the best dressed bus drivers with his bow tie, sharply creased pants and spit shined shoes.

One of the miracles in our marriage was when we first married in 1996, he was making $8.32 per hour, but within a year he was almost at the top RTD driver's pay scale. It took faith for him to ask me to marry him at that rate of pay and faith for me to say yes. But our God had a plan and purpose for us.

After retiring from RTD Ronnie became one of the starters at the Green Valley Ranch Golf Course. As a starter, he would call the golfers to the first tee box over the microphone. He enjoyed that position. That allowed him to play golf for free for many years.

It was also an opportunity for him to influence and help some of the young kids who were just learning the game of golf. Many of them looked up to him and called him Mr. Calloway. He was very well respected. Ronnie played in the Colorado Senior Open several years consecutively. I didn't play golf, but I put together some red and silver Pom Poms and went to the course just before his tee off time and did a cheer for him. "Go team go, go team go. Hit'em High Hit'em Low, Go team Go." Ronnie loved that.

He said, "Jack you're so sweet. I'm going to definitely win now."

He never did win but that was okay. We had fun together and supported each other in everything either of us was involved in or attempted to do.

If Ronnie played golf on Sundays, it would only be after church or whatever his commitment was to God or to me.

I was amazed at Ronnie's consistent commitment to God and His word. He usually got out of bed before I did in the mornings. When I got up I found him at the kitchen table, reading the Bible and taking notes. This practice was almost every morning.

He also had a time when he would go upstairs alone to pray. I often heard him yell out, "Thank you Jesus, Praise you Lord!" It startled me sometimes, but he did that consistently over the years. Ronnie truly loved God and was so grateful for his salvation.

I told the Lord one day, "Lord You sure fixed Ronnie Calloway. That boy has been transformed for real. I love it and I'm reaping the benefits." I'm telling you all of this so you can possibly have an idea of what marriage God's way looks like. In everything give thanks.

When I came downstairs in the mornings he whistled at me real loud and said, "Come over here woman with your fine self and give me some sugar." He Pulled me close to himself and held me real tight while he kissed me passionately on my lips. That happened almost every morning without fail. Even in front of our daughters and grandchildren, my baby was consistent. We knew foreplay begins in the morning.

Ronnie never got tired of telling me how much he loved me. He told me he loved me every single day for the last twenty-four years of our marriage. I never got tired of hearing that and telling him how much I loved him also. Often in the evening while sitting watching television he said, "Have I told you lately that I love you?"

I often said, "Yes you have." He quickly said, "I love you baby." We tried to outdo each other in that regard, but I think he always won. He was determined to win. We both enjoyed the challenge and the kisses.

During the three or four months after we married, I began to look for a job so that I could help Ronnie financially. He told me when he proposed, that I would never have to work another day in my life if I would marry him. I remembered that he choked and coughed when he said that. I had no reason to hold him to that. I was quite capable of working and I wanted to help him.

As time passed, the Lord kept telling me to just stay in the word and continue to listen to Him. Which meant read and pray every morning before I went to look for work or whatever else I would do during the day. It puzzled me that I received a rejection for every position I applied for. I was consistently turned down. I had never had a problem finding a job in Denver before. And yet all doors were closed to me.

We finally figured out that God wanted me to continue to receive instructions from Him and the Bible, so I obeyed. Ronnie was in agreement with that, which was another miracle.

CHAPTER 6

MARRIAGE COUNSELING

When people heard that Ronnie and I had reconciled and married again, they wanted to know how we did that. We started receiving calls asking if they could talk to us. "Of course," was always our reply.

People who knew our history asked me, "How could you forgive him after all of the infidelity?" I told them God requires us to forgive one another according to Matthew 18:18-35 and Mark 11:24-26. I actually opened the Bible and shared with them what it says.

> I assure you and most solemnly say to you, whatever you bind (forbid, declare to be improper and unlawful) on earth shall have (al-

ready) been bound in heaven, and whatever you loose (permit, declare lawful) on earth shall have (already) been loosed in heaven. "Again, I say to you, that if two believers on earth agree (that is, are of one mind, in harmony) about anything that they ask (within the will of God), it will be done for them by My Father in heaven. For where two or three are gathered in My name (meeting together as My followers), I am there among them." Then Peter came to Him and asked, "Lord, how many times will my brother sin against me and I forgive him and let it go? Up to seven times?" Jesus answered him, "I say to you, not up to seven times, but seventy times seven. Therefore, the kingdom of heaven is like a king who wished to settle accounts with his slaves. When he began the accounting, one who owed him 10,000 talents was brought to him. But because he could not repay his master ordered him to be sold, with his wife and his children and everything that he possessed and payment to be made. So, the slave fell on his knees and begged him, saying, "Have patience with me and I will repay you everything. And his master's heart was moved with compassion and he released him and forgave him (canceling) the debt. But that same slave went out and found one of his fellow slaves who owed him a hundred denarii; and he seized him and began choking him, saying, "Pay what you owe!" So his fellow slave fell on his knees and begged him earnestly, "Have patience with me and I will repay you." But he was unwilling and he went and had him thrown in prison until he paid back the debt. When his fellow slaves saw what had happened, they were deeply grieved and they went and reported to their master (with clarity and in detail) everything that had taken place. Then his master called him and said to him, "You wicked and contemptible slave, I forgave all that (great) debt of yours and because you begged me. Should you not have had mercy on your fellow slave (who owed you little by comparison), as I had mercy on you? And in wrath his master turned him over to the torturers (jailers) until he paid all that he owed. My heavenly Father will also do the same to (every one of) you, if each of you does not forgive his brother from your heart." (Matthew 18:18-35 AMP)

I brought these scriptures to people's attention letting them know that Holy Spirit brought these same lessons to my attention. These truths apply to Ronnie and anyone else who may have offended me. Thus, I chose to obey the Scriptures and my Father God. He reminded me that He sent Jesus Christ to forgive me of a debt that I could never repay. Jesus hung on the cross of Calvary in my place. He bled died and rose again from the dead so I could live forever with Him.

Some of the people we were ministering to had never thought of how merciful God has been to all of us in this manner. I brought to many how forgiveness is for our benefit not just for the person who has violated us. I always followed up quickly with Mark 11:24-26 (AMP) because some people don't read their Bible.

For this reason, I am telling you, whatever things you ask for in prayer (in accordance with God's will), believe (with confident trust) that you have received them, and they will be given to you. Whenever you stand praying, if you have anything against anyone, forgive him (drop the issue, let it go), so that your Father who is in heaven will also forgive you your transgressions and wrongdoings (against Him and others). But if you do not forgive, neither will your Father in heaven forgive your transgressions.") I had learned that lesson well and began sharing it with everyone who asked.

Approximately a year after Ronnie and I married, the Lord said to me, "I want you to start counseling people in My Word." I was totally against doing that. I said to the Lord, "I don't want to counsel people. I could be sued for telling someone something that doesn't turn out well for them." Then the Lord reminded me of my words when he delivered me from the alcohol addiction.** Those words were,

> Create in me a clean heart O God; and renew a right spirit within me. Then I will teach transgressors your ways, and sinners shall be converted unto thee.
>
> (Psalms 51:10, 13)

God said to me, "These are the people I want you to teach my ways through counseling. All I want you to do is point them to Me." I thought, wow, I'll be glad to do that Lord. After we received those instructions, we fasted and prayed. With joy, Ronnie and I did relationship and marriage counseling for the next twenty years, giving people the Word of God that He was giving to us. Pointing them to Him. It was all Biblically based with a little bit of experience thrown in.

CHAPTER 7

ANOINTED TO COUNSEL

One thing I have learned in loving and serving Jesus Christ is, what He calls you to do, He equips you to do it. It was intriguing to me when we started to counsel couples, how God anointed both of us to do the work. The anointing was strong on us. It was not a struggle at all and we enjoyed our new assignment.

Ronnie Calloway had found his niche. God anointed him and gave him the ability to share with men who came for counseling. After sharing God's word, Ronnie shared how the Lord had counseled him. It gave me joy to watch him fulfilling his purpose.

For the first several years we didn't ask any payment for our counseling. We were excited to see people receive the word of God and get healed. Plus, along the way we were able to see scores of people accept Jesus Christ as their Lord and Savior, whether they were married or not. That was reward enough for us.

> The fruit of the righteous is a tree of life; and
> he that winneth souls is wise.
>
> (Proverbs 11:30 KJV)

However, later the Lord instructed us to ask for a twenty-five-dollar donation for counseling to the ministry, The Repairer of the Breach as a seed sown toward the healing of their relationships. God also awakened us both one night and gave to us the name of the ministry. He put in our hearts and pointed us to a scripture we had been studying while fasting. Isaiah 58:12 and you shall be called Repairer of the Breach, Restorer of Streets to Dwell in.

Our sessions were usually more than an hour sometimes two hours. We never asked more than the twenty-five dollars which no one ever complained about.

In the counseling process God opened a door for us to have a weekly radio broadcast on KlTT 670 on the dial in Denver, Colorado for eight years. Every Saturday we came on the air for thirty minutes. Our opening song was He's Been Faithful by the Brooklyn Tabernacle Choir. We began our broadcast by saying,

"Hi I'm Jackie Calloway.

And Ronnie said, "I'm Ronnie Calloway. Adultery took me farther than I wanted to go, kept me longer than I wanted to stay, and cost me more than I wanted to pay."

Then I said, "But God has reconciled us first to Himself and then to one another.

We said together,

"We are the Repairer of the Breach Ministry."

After that introduction every week we shared what our old marriage was like with the infidelity and lies and where we are today. Ronnie was more than transparent telling the people why and how he committed adultery. He also shared some of the lies he told me in order to get out of the house to be with other women.

I shared with the people how all of the lies and infidelity affected me and our girls. We talked about how we lived through those first twenty-eight years of marriage which wasn't all bad. Then we shared on every program how we forgave one another making the new marriage possible.

Our focus was mainly on the new relationship and what we went through to get to the forgiveness and reconciliation. We played with each other on the radio. It was risqué. People were able to hear how real our love was for one another. Ronnie said things like, "Girl you are looking mighty sexy today. Is that some new lipstick? We need to hurry and finish this broadcast so I can smear that up a little. Will you let me smear that up?"

I said softly, "Yes."

We became quite famous from the radio broadcast. Famous to some people and infamous to others. One guy actually told us ya'll can't be that much in love. I don't believe it. Our love was true and real, no matter what anyone thought.

Several churches contacted us to do marriage seminars for them which drew large audiences. We were also invited to do seminars across the country and around the world. I also went to Africa and ministered to women and wives In Namibia, South Africa, and Ghana. We were featured on the 700 Club and the OWN network and the program UNFAITHFUL. We were very disappointed in that particular reenactment of our story. They never mentioned Jesus Christ. However, God never wastes anything. One couple who were separated, contacted us for counseling after seeing that program. God put them back together. They asked us to officiate over their ceremony to renew their vows. It was so beautiful to see their marriage restored.

We had thousands to come to our website year after year. Our website was titled "Marriageinspiration.com" which much to our regret got lost somehow on the internet. That website offered forty-eight pages of free marriage counseling. It included help for single persons wanting to marry as well. Also, it was a platform where hundreds of followers contacted us to do seminars on cruises and in the Grand Cayman Islands.

We did our own Repairer of the Breach marriage cruises every year for several years. Ronnie and I actually went on sixty cruises during our last twenty-four years of marriage. We had a twenty-one-day cruise scheduled, that we had to cancel when COVID hit.

Our marriage relationship was for real. Authentic. There was no pretense. We never did phony. I remember telling the radio station manager, "If Ronnie and I ever have an argument before our scheduled broadcast time, I will call you and ask you to play music to fill our half hour." For eight years of broadcasting that never happened.

Ronnie and I were obedient to the Lord's instructions and the Word of God as much as possible. We continued to point people to Jesus until Ronnie went to heaven. The testimony was what attracted people to us. However, the counseling was not based on just our testimony, but the obedience to God's word which they could choose to obey also. The obedience to the Word of God is what we stressed to them, and that helped to heal and deliver them and their marriages. But only if they chose to do the work.

A successful marriage takes a quality decision, by both persons, to commit to do the necessary work. I pray that you will make that commitment today.

CHAPTER 8

LEARNING TO LIVE FOR AN AUDIENCE OF ONE

Almost everyone we knew as well as some we didn't know, had an opinion about who we were and what we were doing. I think it was very difficult for some people to believe that even God could make this marriage happen.

I was talking to a friend one day who asked how was Ronnie doing? I told her he was doing fine. He is in Myrtle Beach, South Carolina playing golf with some of his buddies.

She said, "You trust him to go out of town without you like that?"

I said, "I sure do and it never crossed my mind not to trust him."

She said, "Girl, you're better than me."

I must say that Ronnie had earned my trust over the years since he asked me to marry him. My trusting may have started out shaky, but it was solid now. I trusted Ronnie with my life. He trusted me and both of us trusted God. We learned to live for an audience of one, God almighty. He became more and more our focus. The Holy Spirit did direct our attention to the people, relationships and marriages because that is what He cares about. He loves all of us. No matter what we've done.

Marriage in our culture has become almost passe. Many people don't even know that marriage is not a contract but a covenant. A blood covenant. God intended marriage to be between a man and a woman forever.

Because many people don't follow God's biblical instructions, much of our culture is way off track. Covenant in the Bible in Hebrew infers to cut or to carve. Ronnie and I allowed ourselves to be carved as much as possible to the love of Christ. We allowed the Holy Spirit though His word to carve away from us selfishness, anger, resentment, unforgiveness, and pride. That made it really easy to love each other like we did. I loved him so very much; more than I thought I could have ever loved any human being.

And he loved me back. It was obvious to most people especially to our children that we were actually hot for each other.

In a marriage covenant you both agree to become a servant to your father God and your spouse. It is a complete exchange. This covenant pledges unconditional love and loyalty to God, your spouse and your children. Marriage is total commitment of who you are and all of what you have, in good times and bad times. Most people don't believe that and don't want to hear that. The powerful miraculous Blood of Jesus and the Holy Spirit seals this covenant and helps you fulfill it! That is what we had. I have been loved well. God proved to us that it works.

CHAPTER 9

GOD EQUIPPED US FOR HIS PURPOSE

Ronnie and I were just going along doing what God was instructing us to do. When one of our close friends became ill and was not expected to live. Ronnie and I were on a cruise and when we returned, there were several frantic messages wanting us to call. Our friend Danny was in the hospital. He and his wife Ollie were our daughter Chaunci's God parents. I was shocked to see the condition he was in.

He said to me, "Jackie I want you to preach my funeral."

I said, "Aww no Dad (that is what we called him) you're going to get up from here and you'll be fine."

He grabbed my arm real tight and pulled me closer to him saying, "No, I won't Jackie, but I want you to be the last one to speak over me."

I was shaken by his determination to make me understand what he wanted. His wife Ollie was right there in the room with us and in agreement with his wishes. I was so moved and saddened at the same time.

I said to him, "It will be my honor to do exactly what you ask."

Two days later Danny died. The next day Ollie called and asked me if I would accompany her to the mortuary. I was glad to do so. Everything was paid for in advance but the mortician wanted to know who would do the eulogy.

Ollie said, "Jackie will preach the funeral.

He asked, "Jackie are you an ordained minister?

I answered, "No I'm not but his last request was for me to do his eulogy."

He replied, "You can't do that if you are not licensed."

Ollie spoke up saying, "It was his deathbed request for Jackie to do his eulogy."

The mortician replied, "I'm sorry but she cannot do that."

Ollie laid her hand on mine and said, "It's okay let's go." Well, I was angry. I couldn't believe he was denying my friend his last dying request. I asked Ollie, "Who does he think he is?"

She said, "Don't worry I'm making out the program. I will put you on there and you say anything you want about Danny." She did put me on the program as a special family friend, and I preached before the Minister got up.

The Minister said, "She said she wasn't going to preach, but she did." It was a beautiful service.

Later that week after the funeral I was sharing this incident with my pastor. I told him how that experience had hurt me.

He said to me, "Do you mean you and Ronnie are not ordained?"

I said, "No, we are just doing what the Lord has instructed us to do."

He replied, "I feel led to change that. You have proven yourselves to be faithful ministers of the gospel, under me and I have the authority to ordain you." He did ordain both of us and that was our first ordination. A few years later we were ordained and given license by another ministry that we served.

By the grace and mercy of God almighty, we became marriage pastors Ronnie and Jackie Calloway. Only God could have done that. He equipped us for His service. We served the people for twenty–one years.

CHAPTER 10

GOD OPENS DOORS THAT NO MAN CAN SHUT!

Ronnie and I were continually in awe of what God was doing in marriages and other people's lives. The beautiful thing was that He continually did miracle after miracle in our lives as well. He didn't leave us out.

I told you earlier that when we married Ronnie was making eight dollars and thirty-two cents an hour, but God gave him raise after raise on his job. At first we were living in Ronnie's one bedroom apartment and paying three hundred dollars a month. This apartment was owned by a kindhearted friend who wanted to help Ronnie.

Several months after Ronnie and I were married, while we were busy strengthening the counseling ministry, Ronnie said to me, "Jack, I believe if we go look for a house, God will give us one."

I replied, "I'm in agreement with you brotha. I believe that also." We contacted a realtor and began to eagerly look for a house. Ronnie told the realtor that he wanted to find a house for about $100,000.00. This was in 1998.

The realtor told Ronnie, "Finding a house in this market for $100,000.00 would be impossible for him to find.

Ronnie told him, "I might not be able to find one, but I believe God will find us the very house we need for one hundred thousand dollars."

We looked at homes for a few weeks with him and found nothing. Then my brother called me and said, "I saw a house listed on an index card on the King Soopers bulletin board on Sixth Avenue. You should go check it out."

I thought that is ridiculous. We checked the listing and then the house itself and found a very nice three-bedroom brick home that belonged to a former air force officer. It was located a few blocks from the old Lowry Airforce base.

The day Ronnie and I went to look at the house, the owner just happened to be there. This gentleman had purchased the home by paying the past due taxes. He had completely refurbished this house, and it was beautiful to us. He had redone the original hardwood floors, installed all nearly new appliances and put a washer and dryer in the basement.

We walked through that house and I told the guy, "I believe you fixed this all up for us." Ronnie almost choked when I said that because he knew we had absolutely no money to buy a house at that time. But we believed God.

The gentleman told us that he couldn't sell the house right then because he had to get a quitclaim deed. But he added, "I'm willing to let someone rent to own it in another month or so."

Ronnie spoke up and said, "That sounds good to me. Just give us a month or so to get our house in order and we will talk then." The guy was very nice and wanted us to buy that house.

We left there so excited.

I said, "Ronnie I believe that is our house."

He replied, "Jack we have no money, but I believe God can make this our house." The listing price for the home was $104,000.00. It was God again. However, the next month the gentleman contacted us and offered us the opportunity to rent that house. The rent was seven hundred dollars a month.

The owner said, "A portion of the rent would go toward the down payment on the house."

Ronnie countered saying, "No, all of the rent will have to go toward the down payment or no deal."

The owner reluctantly replied, "Okay." We moved in that next month.

The owner checked our credit and it was approved. That in itself was a miracle. Ronnie had lost the last home we owned in Georgia before we divorced. Then he was homeless for a year. God had miraculously restored Ronnie's credit as only He could have done.

We rented that house for a little more than three years. We received a letter stating that the owner had finally received the quitclaim deed. The closer requested that we come to the closing in two weeks, with five thousand dollars to take ownership of the home. We both looked at each other and laughed out loud.

Then Ronnie took that letter raised it in the air and said, "God just as you have performed miracles in our lives before, we give You the opportunity to perform another one and give us this house."

I agreed in Jesus' name.

We had learned from the Word of God to stay in agreement with each other. The scripture states:

> Again, I say unto you, that if two of you shall agree on earth as touching anything that they shall ask, it shall be done for them of my Father which is in heaven. For where two or three are gathered together in my name, there am I in the midst of them.
>
> (Matthew 18:19 -20 KJV)

Two weeks later we went to the closing with no money. We were all seated at the table with the seller of the property seated across from us.

The closer in charge said, "Mr. and Mrs. Calloway welcome. Because you have overpaid the down payment, we have a check for you for $2,800.00, and we have these papers for you to sign. We were in shock but said nothing.

The owner was stunned and seemed a bit agitated. Nonetheless, we signed the papers and accepted the keys because God gave us that house. But God wasn't finished. The mortgage payment was not seven hundred a month, but six hundred and thirty- five dollars a month. God is Faithful. He is always more than enough. I like to say He is plenty too much.

We lived in that house for approximately four more years. The value of that property appreciated to one hundred and seventy – four thousand dollars. We sold it for our asking price and moved into the house where I now reside.

Year after year God performed miracle after miracle on our behalf always encouraging us to love one another and continue to trust Him in all things. We did that with pleasure.

We had a millionaire who flew us across the country to counsel him and his wife. Their marriage was on the rocks, but God did another miracle. They are still together and blessed today.

There were so many small things that God allowed us to experience that I cherish in my heart. Like Ronnie's calling me on the phone from work singing to me Stevie Wonder's song, "I Just Called To Say I Love You, I just called to say how much I care." He did that so often. There were times I answered the phone and there would be this heavy breathing on the other end.

Ronnie saying, "This is the breather, and I want to breathe in your ear tonight."

I'd respond sternly, "I'm calling the police Mr. breather." Then we laughed out loud together. We laughed a lot together.

I could go on and on about our supernatural love affair that God allowed us to live the second time around. I don't think I'm boring you because it's even exciting to me to recall this marriage God's way. Ronnie and I are *not* special to God. You can have a blessed fun marriage also. All it takes is two people sincerely obeying God's Word.

CHAPTER 11

IN SICKNESS AND IN HEALTH

In the year 2015 there was this big push in our Denver community for men to get medical checkups. Especially African American men. Ronnie never went to the doctor mainly because he was seldom sick. He had never had any surgery.

There was a health fair in Denver and we attended. After having some tests run, the doctor reported to Ronnie that some of his numbers from his blood work were elevated. He suggested Ronnie follow up with another doctor. After several weeks he did see another doctor. The diagnosis was bladder cancer. During one of the examinations, the doctor injured his prostate. Being the man of faith that he was, Ronnie chose to believe God for his healing. Chemo-therapy was out of the question for Ronnie.

Over time Ronnie felt better even after that horrible experience. He was not in any pain or discomfort and we never stopped counseling; we went on with our life.

Cruising was a major part of our lives. Our daughter Rhonda referred to us as "Frequent Floaters" as we were on the sea a lot. Ronnie often said to me, we need a cruise. I was always eager to book us on the newest ship possible. Princess Cruise Line here we come. Or maybe it would be Celebrity Cruise Line or Royal Caribbean. We held platinum status on most of the cruise lines including Carnaval Cruise line. Almost six months after Ronnie's recuperation we went on a cruise. On this particular cruise Ronnie went to the exercise room for his morning workout. He came back to the room and said, "Jack I'm bleeding!"

"What, bleeding?" It was the bladder again. We went to the ship's infirmary. They cleaned him up and inserted a catheter. The doctor couldn't stop the bleeding and insisted that we leave the ship at our next port. Our next port was Victoria, British Columbia. Both of us were afraid. Not only were we far from home, but we were on an Island in Canada we could not fly out of to Denver. Ronnie was still bleeding.

When the ship docked, we were escorted off the ship and given an address to the nearest hospital in Victoria, British Columbia. We were told we could not get back on the ship without a doctor's note saying that Ronnie was well enough to finish the cruise.

We left all of our belongings on that ship. We were bewildered. It was a cold February morning. We walked up this very steep hill together where we found a taxi. Ronnie was pretty weak having bled most of the night.

The taxi took us across town to an unfamiliar hospital where Universal Health Care was the most commonly accepted insurance. The good news is that they accepted our insurance and the clerk checked Ronnie in for treatment. The bad news was they put him in a bed in the hallway because there were no open hospital rooms. I won't go into all of the gory details. It is too painful for me to pen.

Finally, the nurse pushed Ronnie's bed into a small utility room. It was not a regular hospital room. My sweetheart Ronnie bled all day in the hallway until eight o'clock that night. The doctor arrived at approximately eight-thirty p.m. Prior to that time the nurse had emptied several small containers of Ronnie's blood while waiting for the doctor to come.

The doctor was very kind and jovial. He talked to us for a few minutes then examined Ronnie. I told him we are on a cruise and were put off the ship, but cannot return without a signed doctor's permission slip.

He said, "That will be no problem." I felt relieved when he said that. Our only goal was to get Ronnie help, to stop the bleeding and to fly home. We knew we could get a flight home when we got to Vancouver which was our ship's next port. The other concern was our ship was due to sail out of Victoria at 12:00 midnight.

The doctor pulled many, many blood clots out or off of Ronnie's bladder. They were dried old blood clots. He put them in a sink that was in that utility room. These were not the most sanitary conditions I've ever seen in a hospital. The doctor told Ronnie, "It is a good thing they put you off of the ship. These are old blood clots. If these clots had stayed in you much longer, you could have succumbed to blood poisoning."

The doctor finished treating Ronnie, wrote out a prescription which he said we must get filled that night. He also wrote a note for the cruise line stating that Ronnie was well enough to continue the cruise. That certainly was not the truth in my opinion. The doctor wished us well and told us to have a good remainder of our cruise then said good night.

So, praise God we had what we needed. We could now get back to the ship before it sailed. Ronnie sat up with a new catheter inserted and was not bleeding. When he tried to get off of the bed, he passed out. I was able to get under him before he fell to the floor, and I pushed him back up on the bed.

I said, "Ronnie, Ronnie" patting his face.

He opened his eyes and said, "Jack, what happened?"

I said, "Baby, you passed out are you alright?"

He said to me, "I don't know but we have got to get back to the ship." Ronnie then began to have a seizure, shaking all over with his eyes closed. Then he stopped shaking fell limp back on the bed and didn't appear to be breathing.

I panicked calling, "Ronnie, Ronnie wake up." I didn't know what to do but I kept praying, "Jesus, Jesus have mercy." I got up on top of Ronnie and stretched myself over his body putting my mouth on his mouth and he woke up.

He asked, "Jack, what are you doing?"

I responded breathlessly, "Ronnie, you had a seizure and passed out again." He remembered nothing. Just moments after I got off of him, the nurse came in the room.

She said, "The doctor signed your release papers so you are free to go."

I said, "Yes, but Ronnie has lost a lot of blood today and is pretty weak. Do you think you can give him a bag of fluids just to help him on his way?"

She responded, "Sure, that is a good idea because he has lost a lot of blood. I will be right back."

Nobody except the Holy Spirit prompted me to ask that question. I knew absolutely nothing about administering fluids. That thought was just dropped in my mind at that moment. If that nurse had seen what we were doing five minutes before she came in the room, I don't believe they would have released him that night.

The nurse came back gave him the IV fluids and said, "I think we should give him one more bag. What do you think?"

I replied, "I think that's a wonderful idea just to be safe."

She said jokingly, "Mr. Calloway, you're going to get up off of that bed and jog back to that ship." Ronnie said nothing but smiled. When she left the room Ronnie and I held hands and prayed in the Spirit. If you don't know what that means we prayed in tongues. The Scripture says:

> But you, beloved, build yourselves up (founded) on your most holy faith (make progress rise like an edifice higher and higher), praying in the Holy Spirit.
>
> (Jude 1:20 AMP)

That is what we needed to do, build ourselves up on our faith in Jesus Christ and His ability to deliver us in this situation. He has done it numerous times in our lives and He did it again in Victoria, British Columbia. We had victory in Victoria.

After Ronnie finished receiving the second bag of fluids he got on to his feet slowly. We were able to walk to the front desk with no problem. The hospital discharged Ronnie and called a taxi for us. The taxi took us to the dock downtown which was quite a distance from where we had to go. We had to get to the end of the ship where we could board. It was cold outside and Ronnie was weak. He was wrapped in a blue and white hospital blanket the nurse had wrapped around his shoulders to try to keep him warm. He leaned heavily on me as we walked as swiftly as possible.

It was now 11:15 p.m. when we walked up the gang way boarding the ship. Ronnie stood up as straight as possible. I went in front of him and put our room key in the slot. This alarm bell rang so loud, it frightened everyone who was standing nearby. The ship's Captain had decoded our room key which meant they never expected us to return.

Realizing what was happening, I quickly explained to the crew member, that my husband had experienced a medical situation; but we went to the hospital and got treatment. I further explained that we have a doctor's slip stating that my husband is well enough to finish out our cruise. I handed the attendant the note.

He said, "Well, welcome back."

I said, "Ronnie, you go on to our cabin and I will take this note to the doctor in the infirmary."

I knew if the doctor had seen Ronnie after our ordeal and that long hurried walk back to the ship, he may have sent Ronnie back to the hospital that night.

I went downstairs to the infirmary and the doctor was surprised to see me. I gave him the note and he said, "Oh, how is your husband?"

I said, "Oh, Doctor he is so much better, he went on to the cabin to lie down."

He responded, "I am so glad to hear that and glad you were able to see a doctor today. I hope the two of you will enjoy the remainder of your cruise."

"Yes we will and thank you so much for all of your help." The doctor's response was a blessing. It was God again.

My stomach was tight and my heart was beating faster than it had in a long time. The next blessing was that the crew had failed to deactivate our room key. The key was deactivated at the ship's entry, but the key still opened the door to our room. Ronnie was safely in bed. I checked on him then I went into the bathroom put the lid down on the toilet, sat down on it and silently wept. I was still weeping when the ship left the dock. This may have been the most stressful twenty-four hours of my life. As the ship's foghorn blew and we sailed out to sea, I could not stop praising God.

"Thank you Jesus, Praise You Father Bless Your Holy Name. Father You are Great and You do wonderous things. You are God alone, Thank You Jesus!"

Once I composed myself I rested for a short period of time.

Meanwhile Ronnie opened the door and asked "Jack are you okay?"

"Yes love I'm fine are you okay?"

"Yes baby I'm exhausted but I'm going to take a shower."

"Okay love I will stay in here with you." Ronnie was still very weak with the catheter strapped to his right leg.

I sat in the bathroom watching Ronnie shower. I was not going to leave him alone. When he finished his shower, he got back in bed and fell asleep. I showered and quietly cried the entire time. I think I had been traumatized through this harrowing ordeal. But God was Faithful through it all.

I was not sleepy after my shower, so I began to pack our luggage. I packed everything except the clothes we were going to wear home. Ronnie and I agreed when we were in the hospital, we would disembark the ship in Vancouver. Our plan was to get a taxi to the airport and fly to Denver.

Two of our daughters worked for the airlines. I had contacted them when we were in the hospital. We always flew standby.

The next morning Ronnie woke up before me.

When he came out of the bathroom he said, "Jack I'm bleeding again." Once again my heart skipped a beat and tightened.

"I bled overnight and just emptied my bag."

"Baby are you in pain?" I asked.

"No, Jack I'm fine. Let's just get off of this ship and go home."

We disembarked the ship and got a taxi to the airport. When we arrived at the airport I called our daughter Chaunci. Somehow, she arranged for us to get on the next flight to Denver, Colorado. Although we were not side by side on the airplane, we got the last two seats on that flight. I told Ronnie as we boarded the plane, "It's God again." He agreed.

We landed safely after a stress-filled three-hour flight from Vancouver, British Columbia to Denver. Our daughter Rhonda met us at the airport and drove us home.

I asked Ronnie, "Do you want to go to the hospital?"

"No Jack, he answered softly, I'm going to get in bed and pray."

"Okay love, let me know if you want anything. Rhonda and I will be downstairs."

I went downstairs wanting to collapse. I had harnessed my emotions much longer than I ever dreamed I could. I was exhausted. I sat on the sofa looked at Rhonda and let out a long sigh. My only thought was praise God we made it home.

Rhonda asked, "Are you alright Mom?"

I replied, "I really don't know yet. You have no idea what we have been through, and I know Ronnie is not okay. I think he almost died in Victoria."

"Well, now you can eat something and get some rest. What do you want to eat? I can go get whatever you want before I go home."

"Rhonda, I'm not really hungry, I'm going to rest awhile and then check on your father. Thank you so much for bringing us home. I love you and I'll call you later."

"Are you sure Mom? You're going to have to eat something."

"I know but I'll be fine, I just need to rest now and think. The past few days have been difficult and I want to get in bed with Ronnie." I walked her to the door. She hugged me real tight and told me to call her if we needed anything at all. I locked the door went upstairs only to see Ronnie in the bathroom.

I asked, "What are you doing?"

He said," I am taking out this catheter."

I replied, "What?" Without him saying another word he removed the catheter. Immediately there was no more bleeding. Afterward, Ronnie took a shower, put on clean pajama pants got in bed and looked at me. I was left sitting on the bench in our bedroom with my mouth open.

I just looked at Ronnie and he said to me, "Jack, God stopped the bleeding." I closed my mouth took my shower and climbed into bed. We held each other close and drifted off to sleep.

CHAPTER 12

*T*O LOVE AND TO CHERISH

*I*t had become so easy for us to love and to cherish one another. To our knowledge Ronnie had healed completely. We continued counseling couples and individuals daily. Moreover, we were called upon to conduct seminars at churches and on cruises every year.

I recall one special cruise in particular from Los Angeles to Hawaii. On that cruise we celebrated our anniversary and my birthday. It was truly a Love Boat cruise. Ronnie was always romantic, and he did not disappoint on this trip. It was a fifteen-day cruise on Princess Cruise Line. After four days at sea, we docked in Honolulu.

One of Ronnie's classmates from Manual High School, named David, lived there in Hawaii at that time. Ronnie had contacted him prior to our sailing. David met us at the dock in Honolulu. They had not seen each other since high school so it was a special reunion. Ronnie introduced me as his wife, his baby, his sweetheart. From there, they reminisced throughout the morning. David took us to a popular breakfast restaurant there on the Island. The food and service were very good. Ronnie caught David up on the whereabouts of many of their classmates and how they were doing. David hadn't been back to Denver for several years.

David knew that Ronnie had always been a golfer. So, after breakfast, he had set up a free round of golf for Ronnie at the Disney Resort Golf Course. David's son worked there. This thrilled Ronnie so much that he could hardly contain himself. Ronnie had the biggest grin on his face as he rushed to put the rented golf clubs on the golf cart. I thought that was so thoughtful of his friend to do that for him.

After the round of golf David toured us all around the Island. He insisted on taking us to his favorite restaurant for dinner before he took us back to the ship. Our visit with David was marvelous.

On that Hawaiian cruise we also docked in Kauai, Maui, and Hilo. Ronnie and I agreed that the Hawaii cruise was our favorite. We considered it to be a trip of a lifetime. During that trip we renewed and recommitted our love and loyalty to one another. Our relationship was sacred to us. We worked at it knowing that our relationship with God was always the foundation. As we had an intimate relationship with Jesus Christ, we were intentionally intimate with one another. Ronnie and I were also good friends. He was my buddy.

The word cherish is defined in Webster's dictionary as to hold dear, feel or show love for. To take good care of; protect; foster. To cling to the idea or feeling of. Appreciate. Truly, with both of all of our hearts, we cherished one another for twenty-four years.

God blessed us financially with an unexpected windfall. We were free of debt or any added stress. I believe because Ronnie had been homeless during our seven-year divorce, he was very attentive to our household and ministry finances. He always let me know what he was doing, but he handled everything. Neither of us would purchase anything of significance, without the other one's agreement. That kept us in peace financially.

Our marriage was like a dream come true to both of us. Oh, don't get me wrong, we didn't agree on everything.

However, we knew how to get in agreement. We would pray and inquire of the Lord. Plus, we *wanted* to be on one accord with each other.

Ronnie would often say to me, "Jack, can you believe how God has supernaturally blessed us?"

"Love, I see it, we are living it, I'm loving it, so I believe it."

Then he shouted, "Thank You Jesus Praise You Father, thank You Lord."

Ronnie and I continued to give God all the praise and the credit for our lives. We knew our miracle love affair was orchestrated by God. Joyfully, we cherished one another and yielded to His instructions. I encourage all of you married couples to do the same. God inhabits the praises of His people. (Psalm 22:3 KJV)

$\mathcal{H}$OW WILL THIS END?

$\mathcal{R}$onnie and I often asked each other, "How do you think this whole thing will end?"

I said often, "I think I will probably go first. I said chuckling, and I know all the women at my funeral will come hug you and whisper in your ear, "I'm going to bring you a casserole to your house tonight."

Ronnie laughed so hard and said, "I'm only accepting Henri Anna's casserole." Henri Anna is a close friend of ours who always told me that Ronnie was her boyfriend. She thanked me many times for taking such good care of her boyfriend. That was our mutual joke for years. She is happily married to our friend Roy. Ronnie made her and almost everyone he met feel special. Especially the ladies.

I really did think I would go to heaven before Ronnie. Maybe because I didn't want to imagine life without him.

On one cold Sunday morning in October Ronnie turned to me as I awakened and said, "Baby, I'm not going to church this morning, I don't feel so good." This was very unusual for Ronnie. He enjoyed our church and always looked forward to going.

"Are you okay love?" I asked.

"Oh yes I'll be fine, I just think I need a little extra rest today."

"Do you want me to stay with you?" I asked. "Oh no Baby, you go on and just pray for me."

Before I left the house I laid hands on him and prayed for him. He was in good spirits and said he was going to fix himself something to eat.

It had snowed the night before and had started snowing again while I was in church. There was still some snow and ice on the ground, but not very much on the streets yet. Just slush. I was glad to get back home safely. I parked in the garage and came through the kitchen taking my shoes off. I heard Ronnie upstairs. I called out to him while I walked to the livingroom.

"Jack, Baby help me." I looked up to the loft and I could see Ronnie lying on his stomach on the floor. I rushed up the stairs to find him in great distress.

"Ronnie what is wrong Love?"

"Jack, I can't go to the bathroom and look at my stomach." His stomach was very distended like a woman maybe four or five months pregnant.

I tried to help him up but he said, "No Jack." He was only comfortable lying on his stomach.

I said, "Okay I'm calling 911."

Ronnie said, "Jackie please no ambulance you take me to the hospital."

I had connected with 911. The operator heard Ronnie say no ambulance.

She asked, "Can you take him to Presbyterian St. Luke's?"

"Yes I can," I replied.

"The doctor will meet you there in the emergency room. What is his name? She asked."

I told her Ronnie Calloway and I hung up the phone. Ronnie was writhing in pain.

I had not taken off my coat. I helped him down the stairs as gingerly as possible. I got him as bundled up as best I could. He was in terrible pain and could hardly walk.

I was able to get him in the back seat of the car lying on his stomach. It had started to snow heavily again. That meant our ride had to be slow and cautious. I talked to

Ronnie on the way trying to reassure him that he would be okay. He didn't want to talk. He was in too much pain.

We finally arrived at the hospital emergency entrance but no one met us. I went into the hospital and asked if someone could help me?

"I need a wheelchair." A male nurse came and helped Ronnie out of the car. He wheeled him to the desk and the clerk asked, "Do you have insurance?"

I replied, "Yes we do but he needs help immediately."

She said, "Ma'am, I can't do anything for you until I see your insurance card."

I was a bit put off by her but knew I couldn't lose my cool. The agony on Ronnie's face was almost more than I could take. I told the lady that we had called 911 and the operator said that the doctor would meet us here at Presbyterian St. Luke's. She said, "Ma'am you are at St. Joseph Hospital. Saint Luke's is across the street."

I could hardly believe my ears. Ronnie groaned out loud.

I said, "Oh no, how can I get him across the street in this snow?"

The male nurse said, "Ma'am, I will help you, I'll push him over there. You just follow us."

"Oh, thank you so much!" I was so grateful to that young man. The lady at the desk gave me back our insurance card and we left St. Joseph Hospital headed to Presbyterian Hospital. Even though it was across the street, we had to go a city block and a half to get to the correct entrance. It was so cold and still snowing heavily. Ronnie was squirming in that wheelchair while being as patient as he possibly could.

We finally reached the emergency room and a nurse greeted us asking, "Are you Ronnie Calloway?"

I answered, "Yes, yes he is and I'm Mrs. Calloway."

She replied, "We've been waiting for you."

I thanked the nurse who pushed Ronnie to St. Luke's and asked if I could give him something.

He said, "Absolutely not, I'm glad I could help you." I know that was just God showing us favor through that gentleman.

The nurses rushed Ronnie back and they didn't even call for the doctor. They stood him up looked at his stomach and got him up on the examining table. They proceeded to pulled his pants down and inserted a catheter. This was like deja vu for me. I had seen this procedure before. The nurse removed two full liters of fluid from his bladder.

Ronnie was so relieved. He kept saying to the nurses, "Oh, thank you. Thank you so much. Thank you."

One of the nurses said, "How do you feel now?"

Ronnie replied, "Like a new man."

They laughed and said, "Well, we're not finished with you yet new man." They were so nice to us. No one had asked me for an insurance card yet.

The doctor entered and introduced himself. He looked at the chart and talked to the nurses. He examined Ronnie and told him that two liters of fluid had certainly stretched his bladder.

He said, "I think you got here just in time. But this may have injured your kidneys. This was not at all normal. You had to be in a lot of pain. Do you have a urologist that you see?"

"No sir not at the moment," Ronnie answered.

"I will give you a list to choose from, but I want you to see one as soon as possible. Whomever you choose will remove this catheter. But you can easily empty it yourself until then. See a urologist soon. Mainly because you don't want your kidneys to be damaged. If they are damaged, you could be looking at dialysis and you don't want that. The good news about today's episode is that there was no blood in your urine."

Ronnie responded, "Yes sir, I will try to contact someone this week." We thanked him shook his hand and proceeded to the front desk. The nurse put Ronnie back in the wheelchair. I gave the clerk all of our information. I told Ronnie to stay in the waiting room while I went to get the car. However, he insisted on going with me. We hooked arms and started on our walk back to St. Joseph's parking lot. That was a Sunday I will never forget.

On Monday morning Ronnie took the catheter out and he was seemingly fine. I did say seemingly. I could not talk him into going to see a urologist. After his experience with the urologist, who had injured him, he would not go. I didn't want to push him into doing anything that he didn't want to do. Perhaps because I had pushed him to go to the first urologist that injured him.

He rested and stayed at home for about a week. The next thing I knew Ronnie was back to his daily routine with no complaints and ready to go putting the golf ball across the family room floor with seemingly, no problems at all.

CHAPTER 14

WE NEED A CRUISE

Some of you might think Ronnie and I would never want to go on another cruise. Especially after Victoria, British Columbia. Well, that was not true for us.

> For God has not given us the spirit of fear, but of power, and of love, and of a sound mind. (2 Timothy 1:7 KJV)

We had made up our minds that we were going to continue to live and have fun. We cherished each other while enjoying the remainder of the time we had left together. I had become famous among our friends, for being able to find the newest ships on the best cruise lines. In 2019 we actually went on five cruises. Two of them were back-to-back. Ronnie and I got off one ship and boarded another. It was great fun, relaxation and great lovemaking. On two of those cruises, we conducted our ministry Repairer of the Breach Marriage Rendezvous. Several couples joined us.

Ronnie and I have enjoyed dancing together since 1965. We started our courtship on a dance floor. That led to our first marriage. We were able to dance on most of the cruises. It always felt so good for us to hold each other tight while slow dancing. We did a little Texas hop now and then. Ronnie was so cool he only had two good steps. Looking in one another's eyes and laughing gave us joy. I have been loved well. Our last cruise was another Repairer of the Breach Marriage Seminar in February 2020. On those cruises in our Seminars, we encouraged couples to work at laughing and having fun together. Some couples just don't know how to play. One rendezvous theme was Relax, Relate and Release. The couples really liked that one. Intimacy was the thrust of that rendezvous.

Prior to going on the February cruise, we had received information from a home health care company. In light of Ronnie's past health diagnosis, we made some plans. The company informed us that we may be eligible for health care in our home if we ever needed it. This was a possible

benefit from a job Ronnie and I had worked years ago. We were introduced to the owner of the company. She agreed to introduce us to one of their registered nurses; her name is Stacy. Ronnie and I liked her right away. I think we made a spiritual connection with her when we met. Ronnie and I had often talked about home health care because neither one of us have ever been fond of hospitals. We had agreed that when it was our time to go to heaven, we wanted to leave from the comfort of our home.

We had also made out our Living Will and Trust several years ago. However, we knew we had many strong and fruitful years ahead of us.

One of Ronnie's sayings was, "Every day is Christmas with the Calloways." We continued to live that way.

Soon after we returned home from the February cruise COVID hit. Unfortunately, we had another twenty-one-day cruise booked that we had to cancel.

CHAPTER 15

I KNOW HOW THIS STORY ENDS

COVID had caused all travel to cease and we were at home together every day. Of course, that didn't bother us one bit. We were at home together most of the time anyway. The golf course where Ronnie worked part-time was also closed. There were no more calls from people wanting to come to our home for counseling. Our church closed down. We spent many hours talking and loving on one another. We have a huge library of books of varied topics. We did a lot of reading.

On the morning of March 18, 2020, Ronnie got out of bed before me. When I came downstairs he whistled at me really loud as was his custom. I rushed over to him at the kitchen table and gave him a big hug and kiss. We did that consistently. I went on with my day as he continued to study the Scriptures.

Later, Ronnie went upstairs to pray. After a while he called, "Jack, could you come here a moment please?"

"Yes love," I replied in my sexy voice.

I immediately stopped what I was doing and went upstairs. I thought maybe he wanted to play a little bit. I found Ronnie in our bathroom and the toilet was full of blood. My heart sank.

"Oh Love" I said, "What happened?"

He said, "Jack, I haven't been able to empty my bladder fully for the last couple of days, and now this."

"So, what do you want to do Love?" I asked.

"Baby I think we should go to the hospital." Thankfully the bleeding was intermittent. He padded himself up well and put on his jogging suit, his leather jacket and his Bronco leather hat. We decided to go to Presbyterian St. Luke's again mainly because they had treated him well the last time we were there.

The nurses and a doctor attended to him soon after we arrived in the emergency room. The standard treatment was to insert a catheter, drain the bladder and locate the source of the bleeding. Again, nurses were able to remove a large amount of fluid from his bladder. They did a CT scan.

The doctor told us that the bladder was injured and bleeding. Ronnie's blood pressure was very high and they suggested strongly that he be admitted to the hospital. The doctor told us that they just wanted to check his kidneys and make sure they were not adversely affected. They were also concerned about his blood pressure.

When the doctor left the room I asked, "What do you think Dad?"

He responded, "I think I should let them admit me baby, because I am in a lot of pain."

I wasn't surprised this time that Ronnie wanted to be admitted. I could see the worried look in his eyes. He was finally concerned about this bladder condition. Not that he wasn't concerned before, he just didn't trust the medical system.

The hospital sent a young lady to me to make sure all of our insurance information they had was correct. It was a long wait. After a few hours they took Ronnie to a room. The nurse gave Ronnie something to relieve his pain then brought in a bag of saline solution and began to flush his bladder.

I was praying the entire time. We ordered something to eat. Ronnie did eat a sandwich. I could see he was exhausted. I think mostly from the stress of everything. I called the girls and told them he was in the hospital. I planned to stay the night with him. Later that evening the nurse came in and said, "Mrs. Calloway You are able to stay with him until twelve midnight and then you will have to leave."

I responded, "Oh no I'm going to sleep here with him tonight."

She said, "No, you don't understand, you have to leave at twelve tonight because we are shutting down the hospital because of COVID restrictions. Also, you will not be able to return at all." I was shocked to hear that and so was Ronnie. He had never spent the night in a hospital before. Plus, all of his hospital visits had been harrowing. We composed ourselves and began to talk about what we wanted to do.

I said, "Okay I'm sure they will discharge you tomorrow. So, let's just wait and see what they say In the morning."

Needless to say, Ronnie was in the hospital for a week. His condition worsened day by day. We talked on the phone sporadically. He continued to bleed and had seven blood transfusions which I'm not sure were necessary. I was frantic.

He called me at eleven o'clock one night saying, "Jack, pray for me I think they're trying to kill me." Then he hung up suddenly. I called the desk and they didn't answer. I knew the most I could do was to pray. I'm sure they were not trying to kill him.

I contacted Stacy the nurse we had met at the home health care company. She began to intervene sharing with me Ronnie's medical condition. She had more knowledge of the medical terminology, and it didn't look good. Added to his bladder condition he had contracted sepsis. Sepsis is a bacterial infection that spreads through the bloodstream. That infection is commonly picked up in hospitals. His blood pressure was also consistently very high.

The doctors told Ronnie if he did not agree to the surgery they recommended, that he would die.

Ronnie told them, "Well, If I'm going to die, I'm gonna die with my baby. So, since she can't come into the hospital, push me out to the parking lot and she will pick me up."

Our nurse Stacy, called me and told me what Ronnie had said to the doctors. She anxiously told me, "Ronnie has checked himself out of the hospital against doctor's orders."

I wanted to faint but I didn't know how.

She tried to say calmly, "He is waiting for you to pick him up and take him home."

I was speechless. I began to ask the Lord to help me. I didn't know how I could care for him at home as sick as he was.

I was coming out of the grocery store with my friend Andrea when I got this alarming telephone call. Andrea drove me home immediately. I did not put my groceries up. I hurried and got into my car and headed for the hospital. I prayed the entire way there. I thanked the Lord that there is nothing too hard for Him.

"Father, I know I can do all things through Christ who strengthens me. (Philippians 4:13 KJV) Father help me to do the right thing with and for Ronnie. I don't want to injure him in any way. Show me how to care for him and not hurt him." Nonetheless, I was desperately afraid.

It was a cold dreary day in March in Denver. I arrived at the hospital as quickly as possible. Ronnie was seated in a wheelchair just inside the exit door. The nurse pushed him out onto the parking lot to our car. Ronnie was all bundled up in his leather jacket and his Bronco leather hat. He had the biggest grin on his face when he saw me. We passionately but tenderly embraced and held each other for more than a few seconds. I opened the car door and the nurse gently helped him get into the car. Afterward the nurse said to me, "I need your signature on this paper which states that you are taking him against the doctor's orders and the hospital is not liable for his well-being."

I scanned and signed the paper and thanked the nurse.

She said, "Good luck and I wish the best for Ronnie!" I got in the car turned on the heat and we embraced again. Much longer and tighter this time.

Ronnie whispered in my ear, "Baby you look so good and I'm so glad to see you. Oh, I missed you so much." By this time, we were both in tears holding each other. As I am in tears this moment while writing this paragraph and vividly remembering our intimate embrace.

I asked, "Baby how are you doing?" He had lost so much weight and was very pale.

He said in a whisper, "I'm ok baby I'm just glad to get out of that hospital and back to you."

"Are you in any pain, I asked?"

"No, I just want to get home and in my bed." He replied. I know he was in pain. I had loved this man for more than fifty years and I know he was in pain.

We didn't talk much on the ride home. Ronnie could only speak just above a whisper. He was visibly weak. My mind was racing, but I didn't want to overwhelm him with all of my questions.

We entered the garage and I helped him out of the car. I carefully supported him up the stairs into the kitchen. Overcome with emotions, Ronnie wept silently as I walked him into the family room. I helped him remove his jacket and I took off his shoes as he sat in his favorite chair. Ronnie was very emotional thanking God for being home.

He said, "Jack, The house looks so nice." Ronnie was always particular about a neat and clean house. I smiled as I sat on the floor at his feet. We paused looking at each other while enjoying one another's presence.

Soon he said to me, "Baby, I think you'll have to help me upstairs now. I need to lie down."

We climbed the stairs slowly together. Ronnie clutched the banister with one hand, and put his arm around my shoulders with the other. He was terribly weak and could hardly put one foot before the other. I was not afraid anymore. I believe having him in my arms calmed me. Also, the Spirit of God embraced us. God's peace was and is always present in our home.

I got him undressed as he let out a deep sigh while stretching out in our bed.

"Thank you Jesus, he whispered. Oh, this feels so good to be at home and in my bed."

Ronnie had a Foley catheter inserted, and it was full of blood and blood clots. I emptied it. I took note that he had a high fever. He was very hot. I put cold wash cloths on his forehead and under his neck. I also placed small wrapped ice packs on the bottom of his feet as he drifted off to sleep. I was not afraid, but I sure didn't know what I was going to do. The first thing that came to my mind was to continue to pray. I did that as I sat by our bed holding Ronnie's hot feverish hand.

"Lord Jesus I ask that you heal my baby and show me how to care for him. In Jesus's name I pray." As my prayer ended, Stacy called and said that she would be here to help me soon. That was the answer to my prayer. Stacy came about an hour later and went right to work.

She said, "You both have been approved for the health care services and my boss has given me permission to help Ronnie."

Tell me something people, "Is God good or what? He is always more than enough."

She said, " We will have to irrigate his bladder to prevent the blood clots from building up. This has to be done frequently. I will do it now, but I will show you how to do this also."

I went into nurse's training at that moment. Stacy was my teacher; hence, I became a nurse. My only credentials were a deep Love for my husband and faith in God that I could help him. By the grace of God, I did help him. I learned if you ask the Lord to give you the ability to learn what you need to learn, He will do that. Couples, don't ever under estimate God's ability to supply all of your need according to His riches in glory by Christ Jesus.(Philippians 4:19 KJV) That Scripture covers whatever you need, not just finances. Knowledge, stamina and perseverance are included.

The book of James states, If any of you lack wisdom, let him ask of God, that giveth to all men liberally, and upbraideth not; and it shall be given him. (James 1:5 KJV)

To all you married couples, don't limit yourselves to only what you think you can do. God's ability is limitless with and for you if you believe and trust in Him.

Stacy was at Ronnie's bedside until after midnight that night. She set up everything that I needed. She explained to me what I needed to do and at what time I should complete the procedure.

I was to continue to take Ronnie's temperature. When he awakened after Stacy left, his temperature was 101 degrees. We had work to do. Ronnie would wake up off and on during the night. He was clearly not comfortable; but thank God he was not in any pain. The next morning when he awoke he gave me a big smile realizing he was home and in his own bed.

"Good morning baby," he whispered.

"Good morning love," I replied. I'm going to bring a pan of water to you; so that you can wash up and brush your teeth and then I can give you a big kiss. He smiled and whispered, "That will work. I need that kiss." Stacy came soon after I had gotten Ronnie all cleaned up and changed his pajamas. His temperature was now 100.6 degrees. She tended to him while I cooked breakfast. This pretty much became our daily routine.

The bleeding and clotting continued. Nurse Stacy connected Ronnie with a new doctor an oncologist from another hospital. Ronnie really liked the new doctor. He asked her if she was a Christian and she said yes. That fact helped him trust her a little more.

Many days I called Stacy. If she couldn't come, she talked me through the process of whatever we were going through that day. The health care company supplied us with all the medical supplies we needed. Of course, our children were there to see dad every day. That certainly helped his recovery.

The next few weeks were touch and go. He was a very sick man and we all knew that. Ronnie asked me to read the scriptures and pray over him every day and at night. He also had Christian television broadcasting in our bedroom. He watched teachings on healing and life. Ronnie read as much as he could. Unfortunately, he was sometimes too weak and lethargic.

I learned to irrigate Ronnie's bladder day and night. Pulling those blood clots through the tube into the catheter bag. That was a delicate procedure for me and for him. I didn't want to do anything that would hurt him.

Finally, Ronnie began to slowly improve. He was now sitting up in the bed and giving orders. The home health care people sent in another nurse. Her name is Lynette. She administered medications and did the irrigation of the bladder. She also bathed Ronnie every day. At one point he had round the clock twenty-four-hour nursing care. God supplied all the help we needed. We prayed like we never had before.

However, as he started to get better, he didn't want people in his house at night.

Ronnie said to me, "Jack, I love you so much, and you know I'm just used to taking care of you."

"I know Dad, but you'll be back on your feet real soon. I love the way you take care of me too. I love the way you love me. You're the best!"

It took three months for Ronnie to get back on his feet again. It was a lot of love, professional nursing and the healing power of God. Nurse Lynette worked diligently with Ronnie and me. She is part of the family now.

I can truly say, Ronnie Calloway had the best care possible. He improved gradually. We wanted to find that doctor who told Stacy that Ronnie could bleed out on the way home from the hospital and die. I wanted him to see the miraculous power of God. I'm sure Ronnie could have bled out considering the condition he was in the day he left the hospital. Needless to say, God had another plan. A wonderful plan.

CHAPTER 16

REMARKABLE IMPROVEMENT

Ronnie miraculously regained his strength. I was amazed at his progress. He was no longer bedridden. My sweetheart was excited to be able to come downstairs and have his meals at the kitchen table. He was now strong enough to shower by himself and putt around the house with his golf clubs. I think going on the golf course was what he missed most. I won't go into all of the details, but Ronnie Calloway recovered. God is so good and we were giving Him all the Praise and all the Glory.

It became more and more difficult to keep Ronnie in the house. He was ready to go out on his own. I wouldn't let him go at first. Then I saw there was no stopping him. Lynette had a hard time nursing him anymore. I was thrilled to see him almost himself again.

I had learned so much during those past three months. I already knew I loved Ronnie Calloway with all of my heart. But my love deepened and became stronger. I was able to do things for him I never dreamed I could. I have never had a strong stomach. In the past, the sight of blood would cause me to leave the room one way or another. For Ronnie I have delt with more blood than I've seen in all of my life. I have run up and down two flights of stairs at his whimper in a single bound. I became super woman lifting and moving whatever necessary.

The phrase we stated in our wedding vows in sickness and in health comes to my mind. I don't think many of us think about that sickness part when we repeat those vows at our weddings. Some couples take those words out of the wedding vows. I've come to see how important those words are. I believe couples should think about the possibility sickness might show up in your marriages. I challenge you to ask yourself how you might respond.

I learned also God can give you strength and stamina, beyond your natural ability. Just ask and believe Him for it. Often we grow and mature in times of adversity. Trials don't always present themselves from outside of the marriage. Sometimes they show up in your midst and when you least expect them.

I counsel you and others I know to live prepared. The greatest preparation and security I know is to have an intimate daily relationship with Jesus Christ. He will always be there for you no matter what the situation. Jeremiah 33:2-3 (AMP) states:

> Thus says the Lord Who made the earth the Lord Who formed it to establish it the Lord is His name: Call to Me and I will answer you and show you great and mighty things, fenced in and hidden which you do not know (do not distinguish and recognize, have knowledge of and understand).

That Scripture right there is more than enough for me. I witnessed Him doing just that for me in the last three months. He has proven Himself and His ability to me since I was a child. I knew exactly who to call on because He is and always has been faithful and more than enough for me and Ronnie. He wants to be the same for you if you trust Him.

CHAPTER 17

*F*ROM THE OUTSIDE LOOKING IN

*O*ur marriage and reconciliation have always been on display for the last twenty- four years. God planned it that way. We have been on national television, local radio and done seminars across the world. The Cayman Islands, Africa and passengers on cruise ships have heard and welcomed our testimony. I want to share with you some of the observations and testimonials our friends and family have made about our relationship and marriage.

❧

My family and I have been blessed to have Ronnie and Jackie Calloway in our lives for the past 20+ years. When my husband and I met them, we both knew it was a divine connection that only God could have done. A true love and Godly relationship began to quickly develop between the four of us.

Due to the love, support, wisdom, and mentorship that naturally developed over time, the Calloway's became our Spiritual Parents. In addition, we asked them to be the "God-Grand Parents" for our daughter who was born in 2005! Over the years it was apparent why God connected us with the Calloways. We received marriage, parenting, and individual counseling including much more support we could never put into words. I have personally watched both Jackie and Ronnie not just talk the talk but walk the walk when it comes to living life God's way. I can recall several times hearing Dad Calloway say, "I can't give you anything but the word of God!"

Whenever we had the blessing to be in their presence, we would witness the true LOVE they had for one another. I have yet to see other couples express their love towards one another in such a true, authentic, genuine way. Dad Calloway would whisper sweet nothings in Mom Calloway's ear, and she would laugh like a teenage girl being courted by her boyfriend. It was the cutest thing to witness. Also, when we had the pleasure to travel with them and attend marriage seminars or special events hosted by

"Repairer of the Breach Ministries," we would experience testimonials, teachings, and revelation from God. It is apparent why God called Ronnie and Jackie Calloway to preach the Gospel to the Nations. God has truly been glorified because of their obedience and love for Jesus Christ our Lord and Savior.

Evangelist Linnea Hutt

⚘

I don't remember exactly when I first met the Calloways but it was one of those experiences that you say, there is something special about them. I realize that something was love. A genuine love for each other, a genuine love for God, a genuine love for people to know God's love and that they needed a Savior. Throughout their testimony they were sure to acknowledge God and Jesus Christ as the reason for their rekindled love for each other. They demonstrated an openness and transparency into their marriage and what God did to bring them back together. In doing so they wanted everyone to know that whatever circumstances, heartbreak, loss, hopelessness you may experience that Jesus will help you through it. They were not a couple that just spoke the message of God's love but lived it. The Calloways were a Godly example of a couple being married God's way. They weren't perfect, but they walked in integrity and compassion. Not compromising on God's principles but living the Word. I spent time with them together and individually. Both would be quick to tell you of their first love Jesus Christ and their second love was for each other. I have known many Godly couples but there's not many who have impacted my life, my marriage, my walk with God as much as Ronnie and Jackie Calloway. Good and faithful servants, well done!

Elder Adrian Hutt

∽

My parents were so much one in both the old and new marriage. When Mom gave instructions or an answer to my sister and I, I heard Dad's voice. When Dad gave instructions or an answer, I heard Mom's voice. It was made perfectly clear that there was no playing them against each other. I call this parenting God's way! When I was a little girl I would dream of marrying a man like Dad and being a wife and mother like Mom. I watched my parents play hard and pray harder. My dad whistling, gazing, and gawking at Mom, and Mom holding dad's hand and tummy and kissing him. That was the norm. I also witnessed them go to war together on their knees in agreement; for every situation in life.

It is rare that a template or an example of a Godly marriage is exhibited. Mom and Dad's marriage was that template for me. Their life was so much louder than their talk. God was the author and finisher of their marriage. I saw first-hand what a marriage God's way looks like.

Rhonda Calloway Williams

⁂

A picture is worth a thousand words. In all of our family pictures you can see the love that Mom and Dad had for each other. Dad loved to call Mom's name. Whether the deck was on fire or Dad was wanting Mom to come and look at something, he would always call her name. I can hear him now, "Jack, Jack!"

He has left this earth but I still hear him calling her name. I miss you Dad.

Chaunci Calloway

∾

My favorite part of Uncle Ronnie and Aunt Jackie's story is seeing their love the second time around. Being their niece and only ten years younger, I was able to observe them as a couple in my youth as married and divorced; not understanding a lot of what I was seeing, then as a maturing married woman. Their Part 2 was of ever increasing love that truly became a visible demonstration of the love of God. Forgiveness, kind words, commitment, the oneness that grows from respect and sacrifice yet with playful endearing touches and Song of Solomon like looks; they became a picture of the blessing and fulfillment only found in Christ. In humility and faith they believed God and said, "YES" to the opportunity to be examples of a marriage without regrets. I love you (Uncle Ronnie) Aunt Jackie.

Rhonda Brown

⤢

My wife Marti and I met Ronnie and Jackie Calloway in 2007 when we joined the Church they attended. They shortly embraced us as members of their own family. As such, I've had the privileged opportunity to see first-hand how they exemplify marriage God's way. However, it was obvious to anyone who spent any time with them, that their LOVE for God and LOVE for one another was how they exemplified marriage God's way.

You could see it every time Ronnie would run to open a door for Jackie as she patiently waited in expectation. You could see it in how Jackie honored and respected Ronnie and carried herself as the virtuous woman he was proud to call his wife. He vowed to do whatever it took to please her and she was his helper in becoming the man of God he was called to be.

I'm thankful for their example of marriage God's way. I'm especially grateful for how Ronnie exemplified marriage God's way from a male perspective, for the benefit of myself and many other men as well. Thank God for Marriage God's way"!

Mr. Reney DuBose

⚬⚭⚬

Jesus painted the ultimate picture of what forgiveness looks like, and yet we rarely end up seeing it displayed in front of us. Whether it's how we treat one another, or how we see others treat each other. The true act of forgiveness seems so far out of reach, even within the Christian community. Often we simply say we forgive each other without actually taking the steps to reconcile that trust, or covenant which was breached.

Ronnie and Jackie Calloway are one such couple that not by words only, but by deeds showed my husband and I that forgiveness, reconciliation, and restoration of the marriage covenant is possible, as are all things through Christ. They showed us walking out the act of taking pause when answering your spouse so as to display love and patience. They showed us forgiving one another is to truly be like God, not remembering the sins of the other. But one of the greatest lessons we learned was to challenge ourselves when we have the opportunity to be offended by our spouse. They taught us that we can refuse to take offense. They showed us how that act of mercy and grace ripples through a marriage and leads to true forgiveness of offenses.

We will always be thankful for their obedience and spiritual guidance. Their unwavering commitment to displaying what true Godly forgiveness looks like in a marriage.

Bridgette and Jimmy Montecinos

∾

I was at the building where I used to pastor when I saw Pastor Ronnie heading to the barber shop on Fairfax Street in Denver, Colorado. He was holding Pastor Jackie's book. We engaged in small talk and during our conversation he said, "I was placed on this earth to make Jackie happy."

Pastor Rene Townsell

∾

God gave me an upfront, close and personal, eye witness account of God's Love in Motion, God's way! Through my observation of the second and final marriage of my spiritual God parents Ronnie and Jackie Calloway, I learned:

- Marriage is the will of God!
- Marriage is created by God!
- Marriage is covered by God!
- Marriage is important to God!
- Marriage is protected by God!
- Marriage is unity with God!
- God's purpose for marriage is unity! Where there is unity, God commands the blessing! (Psalm 133:1)

Lastly, I make the analogy of marriage to a dance. In the lyrics of a great song titled, I Hope You Dance, by Mark D. Sanders and Tia Sillers it says, " And when you get the choice to sit it out or dance. I hope you dance... I hope you dance! Thank you Mom and Dad Calloway, you gave me hope and I choose to dance!

Pastor Felicia (Lisa) Smith

◦◦◦◦◦

My Buddy Ronnie always spoke about Jackie in glowing words. How foxy she is, a corny term, but I knew what he meant. Whenever he talked about her there was a sparkle in his eyes. He had this smile on his face that other men recognized as his girl was sur- nuf, sur-nuf.

When playing golf, he talked about, "I can't wait to see my baby." After a round of golf, we would be having refreshments, and if he didn't have his phone he would borrow mine to call home. His favorite phrase was, "Hey Baby."

In all the times Ronnie and I were together, I never heard him say a disparaging word or phrase when he talked about Jack. He recounted the many memories they had on their cruises. Exploring the Islands while on shore, making love in their cabin, nothing descriptive just a sweet remembrance. Ronnie left no doubt how he felt about Jackie his fine wife in thought word and deed.

Mr. Preston Anthony

∽

I was fortunate to witness a love that was truly love God's way. When a man loves outwardly without being worried about judgment, he is definitely in love. I was Ronnie's barber for years and I always admired how he told any and every one about how much he loved God and his wife. People who never met Jackie, knew her through Ronnie's love for her. Jackie set such a tone for a righteous marriage that Ronnie had to respect in order to be one with her. He often told me Jackie was a woman of God. The first time I met her I could tell right away what she stood on. They were so kind and gentle with one another. So clearly when God said love is kind and patient, I observed that with them all the time. They were very encouraging and team players for one another. If God had an example of what marriage should look like, it would be their marriage front page. I was honored to have witnessed how two humans that God created different could come together and Demonstrate a love that God designed.

Mrs. Shawn Harrell

⚭

I remember Mr. & Mrs. Calloway's marriage being pretty much perfect. When Mr. Calloway would invite me to go golfing, I was a little boy at the time so my mom would drop me off at their house sometimes early in the morning. I would sit in the living room with a glass of water watching golf on the television. Of course, not really knowing how golf worked but attempting to understand it. I would listen to the conversations they had between each other. It was always calm and positive, filled with love and attention. Mr. Calloway would add in bits of humor giving Mrs. Calloway, what I felt was reassurance, and seeing her smile was icing on the cake.

Mr. Calloway was a person I looked up to for many reasons. How he treated and respected his wife Mrs. Calloway was one of the main reasons. Genuinely making her laugh and smile in everything he said and did. Mrs. Calloway was the same with him. Making him giggle or blush, it was always love and humor between both of them.

I appreciate those interactions I was able to be a part of. The sweetness they shared with each other gave me a perspective of how marriage should be and definitely something I'll be bringing into mine. I love them both simply because it is rare to ever see real genuine love between two people anymore. They both are my reminder that it is very much possible to still obtain something so special.

Mr. Troy Davis Jr. (Age 23)

⚬⚬⚬

There is so much I could say about the Calloways. But a life-changing memory for me is when I was in a very abusive marriage and was doing some counseling in their home with Pastor Jackie. Pastor Ronnie strolled through the room with a smile greeted his wife and my self. He saw the tears and hurt on me. We started talking and he started speaking life back into me. Things like how a king treats his queen. How God sees me and I was the prize in marriage.

I believed every word because I saw him walk the walk with his wife. From that day I started picking myself up and walking that pain out of me. Until this day his example of a mate is always at the forefront of my mind. If it ain't like that, I don't want it!

DeeDee Rockette

☙

Ronnie and Jackie Calloway truly exhibited a supernatural bond. They showed what it meant to be bonded as one. My personal experience was seeing these two share one cell phone. Now you might be saying well that's not so supernatural, but try sharing a phone with your significant other. The level of communications, trust and bonding one must have to share in all levels of their lives. What one knew, the other either knew or would know. (sic) Ronnie and Jackie shared a unique bond and a beautiful example of a marriage that was based in Christ and exhibited as an example for us to see God's power working in the lives of two people that loved Christ and trusted God in all things.

Andrea Mosby

☙

Ronnie and Jack's (as I call her) second marriage was seen as a testimony to the bond of their first marriage. I never acknowledged the "in-between stuff." Their ongoing commitment to helping married couples through troubled times with Faith based principles and practices, were as practiced within their own marriage. They seemed to understand the importance of focusing on their personal and marital growth as they were assisting in the growth of those they counseled. Their faith and reliance on the Lord were demonstrated in how they honored and supported each other in their journey together.

Ronnie was a few years ahead of me in school. We met at City Park Golf Course, when I was a preteen. We were there to caddy, Ronnie would be putting on the putter's green, while we waited to be chosen. He shared his teen wisdom with me, like:

What makes a man smart.

You aren't smart unless you know Jesus.

How to be nice to young ladies.

The importance of keeping your shoes shined.

Your clothes neat

Your fingernails clean

I've known Jack since my late teens. They have been cherished friends and always made me feel welcomed when I stopped to see them.

They are Auntie and Uncle to our children and Brother and Sister to me.

Dennis Irvin

◦⤬◦

Wow, where do I begin? I have known Ms. Jackie and Mr.

Ron for almost 20 years. I didn't know anything about Mr. Ron's life before I moved next door to them. I began to learn about Mr. Ron's life when I read Ms. Jackie's book, Love That Would Not Let Me Go. After reading the book I was like, o boy. This isn't the same guy that I know.

Mr. Ron told me a few stories about himself and his relationship with Ms. Jackie. One story I will always remember, he told me that he was living proof that God can do anything. He told me that if he didn't have Ms. Jackie in his life he didn't know how he would go on.

During my observation I knew this was true. Especially when I saw the flowers he would buy her. He would open the doors for her and there were times he would provide her with limousine rides. You could feel the love and see their happiness when you were around them.

Kids today would say the love and affection he showed Ms. Jackie was goofy. I can truly tell you this was far from being goofy. I always admired his love, commitment, and his swagger. To me this made him a very cool guy. I've seen a lot of relationships but not quite like theirs. I must admit that I was a little jealous in a good way. Observing their relationship made me work harder on my relationship.

All I ever saw was unconditional love and I would always think to myself, It takes a real strong man to do and say the things that he did. In the end I realized he was a man of God and he did not let his past dictate his future with his beloved wife Ms. Jackie.

Mr. Kevin Thomas

∽

I remember Aunt Jackie spending time with us in Lansing, Michigan one summer. We had to pick up Uncle Ronnie at the airport and she was so excited.

I must have been in my teens or early twenties when she said, "I have to brush my teeth, I know he's going to want to kiss me. She was right! They fell into each other's arms and kissed. I thought, I want that! I saw such love.

I couldn't wait to experience a loving marriage like they had. Seeing a couple who actually enjoyed each other made me want it even more. I miss seeing them together, and have always said they were my hero's and my inspiration.

Roslyn Riddle

∽

Even as a young man, I saw my grandparents love one another well. I saw the way my grandpa would marvel at the mention of Jackie Calloway. I saw the true desire to want to learn more and more about her every day. I saw my grandma's love for him grow as he became ill. She did things that she never thought she could do and quite honestly wasn't equipped to do. But because of her vows, for better or for worse, because of the strength that she gained from the Holy Spirit, and just simply because she loved Ronnie Calloway, she was supernaturally equipped.

Azlan Williams

⸎

From back in the day when I was a teenager showing up to our teenage Bible study, Sensitizing Ourselves Spiritually, while intoxicated. S.O.S was the Bible study Mrs. Calloway had started for the teenagers in our church. To this present day, you allowed me to be your stylist. I thank God that I've had the opportunity to be a part of and share so many amazing memories with you and Mr. Calloway. I remember the many times it took everything in me to forgive people and forget the offense. You both encouraged and pushed me to do things I never thought I was capable of doing.

I'm proud to call you my spiritual parents. There has never been a time when you weren't on my heels teaching me that when you know better, you should do better.

When it comes to love, no one compares to you. Whenever I saw you, I saw him. Worshiping and praising God, hugging, kissing, dancing…you guys were always together enjoying each other. I remember asking myself, is this what love looks like? I want that kind of love. I want my husband to love me as much as he loves the Lord. I want my cheeks to hurt from smiling when my husband walks into a room and sweeps me off my feet. I want the kind of love that even when I'm not with my husband, I can still feel his love with me. That's what you call that Calloway kind of love. Thank you for loving each other authentically. Never fake, never extra and never too much. Troy and I are a better couple today because you allowed us to watch and experience your love. For that I am forever grateful. I appreciate you and I love you with my whole heart.

Mrs. Tonya Davis

⚬⚭⚬

A Marriage with God at the Helm. In April of 2020, I had my first encounter with Jackie and Ronnie Calloway. Ronnie had just come home from the hospital and was weak and de-conditioned. That means he was not at 100% capacity to perform daily functions. I stopped by their house for an interview as they needed to approve of me prior to me providing care. When I entered their home, I noted it was beautiful and serene. There was a sense of peace in the house. After greeting Jackie, I was escorted to meet Ronnie, and he spoke with me for about an hour. We exchanged some pleasantries and then Ronnie asked me if I knew Jesus? I was happy to report that I did. A session of Q & A followed and when asked if he would like me to come back again, I remember him saying, "You'll do." With Jackie's agreement, I was to begin spending time with this wonderful couple. After a few days with them, Jackie told me that she had prayed to God for me. I felt honored and looked forward to every encounter with them.

Watching Ronnie and Jackie was one of the most precious experiences of my life. Every day with them was a blessing. I remember so many things about them, but space allows for just a few of those moments.

One afternoon, Ronnie and I were talking about something and he referred to a passage in the Bible, which was the bulk of our conversations, and he stopped and said, "Jackie knows where this is." He raised his voice to reach her ears, mentioned something very specific that was in the Bible and Jackie immediately told him where that particular passage was. He looked at me and smiled, nodding his head as if to say, 'I knew she'd know.' They were always referring to revelations they had that they discovered in The Word.

One time, some friends stopped by from out of town and while talking with them, Jackie laughed. I saw her looking at Ronnie and I asked what he said that made her laugh? She looked at me and said, "I just love him." He had not said anything. Looking at him filled her with so much joy, she was giddy. The idea that simply looking at someone else could cause so much joy that laughter broke out, was new to me. Another time, there was nothing specific happening and Ronnie walked over to her and put his hand out. Jackie stood and they just started dancing in the middle of the room. They danced for no reason other than they loved each other and wanted to be close to each other.

I was blessed to see their love from the front row. God was involved in every detail; it was pure joy to witness and learn how to do marriage God's way.

Nurse Lynette Gilbert

∽

The point of this chapter is not to glorify Ronnie and myself. It is to make you aware that there are probably people who are watching you and your marriage. With this knowledge you have the wonderful opportunity to point others to Jesus Christ and to show them a marriage God's way.

Father God, I believe what you wanted to accomplish by reconciling Ronnie and me has been accomplished. The world has seen your power, your glory and your love!

Thank you for allowing us to be your little funnels. Little funnels that you poured your love through to other people.

CHAPTER 18

ONLY DEATH COULD PART US

My husband had recovered to the point of feeling young again. He felt young enough to buy himself a convertible Jaguar. I thought wow, he's back. However, he was still under the doctor's care. We still had nurses Lynette and Stacy when they could catch up with him. Nonetheless, he was feeling so much better. I was thrilled, and I began to relax with him. We were inseparable and loved each other more passionately than ever, never failing to say to one another what was on our hearts. We always had in the forefront of our minds that tomorrow is not promised to us.

Ronnie had become confident in his ability to put the thought of sickness behind him. He was back doing all that Ronnie does. He ironed sixteen of his dress shirts one morning. That same day he cleaned out the garage, swept the kitchen floor and cooked our dinner.

During this time, he said to me, "Jack, I want you to have a new kitchen." He let me pick out a new stove, refrigerator, dishwasher, backsplash and new flooring. Of course, I let him have some say in the choices.

Things were going very well. We were dating again not that we ever stopped. Ronnie took me out to dinner and lunch often. He didn't want to sit across the table from me but close beside me. He was the ultimate lover. The intimacy between us strengthened our union, and kept me feeling young and special. I believe it will do the same for you and your relationship. I challenge you to touch and hold one another as often as possible and on purpose. God wants to bless you spirit, soul and body, but you must put forth a consistent effort. Husbands, love your wives and seek the highest good for her and surround her with a caring, unselfish love, just as Christ also loved the church and gave Himself up for her. Wash her with the water of the Word of God. Wives be subject to your own husbands as a service to the Lord. Respect and honor him and always speak well of your husband. You can read more specifically about those instructions from the word of God in Ephesians 5:22-33 (AMP).

One day Ronnie went to the gym to build his strength. He worked out but did too many leg lifts. Regretfully, the bleeding started again. Afterwards Ronnie had difficulty walking.

Reluctantly, Ronnie was forced to slow down. Actually, he had to halt all of his activities. The loss of strength in his legs and the bleeding left him no choice but to be at home. At first he was angry at himself for over-doing his exercise. For the first time in months, he complained to me of pain in his legs and back. It happened so fast. Overnight, we went from riding in his convertible across town to back at home bleeding again.

One morning I fixed Ronnie breakfast as he sat at our kitchen table. The table is a high glass table with high chairs. Our feet don't touch the floor while sitting in these chairs. I had just put Ronnie's plate in front of him when suddenly he had a blank stare on his face and his mouth hung open.

I yelled, "Ronnie, Ronnie!" He began to fall over from the chair. I quickly positioned myself under him while helping his limp body gently to the floor as best I could. I continued calling loudly Ronnie, Ronnie. I pulled the phone from the counter and dialed 911 while lying under him. I let him down gently on the floor. I rushed to open the front door as I was instructed to do by the 911 operator. I returned quickly to Ronnie on the floor as he began to come around. Praise God the fire department is just around the corner. An ambulance was here in five minutes. The emergency medical personnel rushed in and began to talk to him. Ronnie was confused and asked me what happened.

I answered, "Ronnie, I think you may have had a seizure or a TIA, a mini stroke."

By this time the attendants had taken his vitals and put him on the gurney rolling him toward the ambulance outside. Ronnie and I were still in our robes. They got him in the ambulance, and I heard a loud, "Jack, Jack." I literally ran out to the ambulance in my robe and slippers.

Ronnie said, "Jack don't let them take me to the hospital."

He looked at the attendant who was trying to give him an I. V. and said sternly, "I am not going anywhere. Let me out of this ambulance."

The attendant answered, " Sir, the only way I can let you out is if you answer three questions. "Who is the President of the United States? What year is this? and something else?" I don't remember the last question but Ronnie answered them all correctly.

About that time Stacy, his nurse, showed up unexpectedly. We were not expecting her that morning. She talked to the EMTs and they let him out of the ambulance. By this time all of our neighbors had gathered around.

As we walked back into our house Ronnie raised his hand and said, "Okay folks, I'm fine you can go back home now. Love ya!" He was all smiles. I was still in shock, in my robe and shaking my head.

Stacy insisted that he lie on the sofa while she took his vitals and asked, "What in the world happened?" I explained everything to her while Ronnie rested and listened. He didn't remember what had happened himself. Stacy said it sounded like he may have had a TIA. She explained to us that a TIA is defined as a Trans Ischemic Attack or a mini stroke. She did talk Ronnie into going to the hospital just to get checked out. He reluctantly agreed to go to a different hospital, not the hospital he had previously checked himself out of. A physician examined him thoroughly in the emergency room and released him to return home.

In a matter of weeks, he was bedridden again. Thank God Lynette and Stacy were back on their posts. Oh, I was back on my post also. Don't get it twisted. I was there with him for every turn of events. The Foley catheter had to be inserted again. The irrigating of the bladder resumed.

This setback was different for Ronnie. He was hopeful for recovery, but disappointed to be as sick as he was. I assured him that he would be fine. We prayed together daily. He seemed to pray without ceasing. I know God was talking to him consistently.

One Saturday morning I had cooked breakfast for Ronnie. He wanted pancakes. I helped him out of bed to sit in the chair in our bedroom. I set up the television tray in front of him and we began to talk while he ate.

Suddenly, Ronnie had this blank stare and his body went limp. I called, "Ronnie Ronnie," but he was sliding to the floor. I moved the tray and eased him to the carpeted floor and called 911 again. Unlike the last episode he woke up before they arrived. I got him back into bed and he seemed to be fine again. I called Stacy this was another TIA or mini stroke.

Ronnie got weaker and weaker as one month passed. He had regular visits to the oncologist. She took very good care of him. He liked her a lot and she liked him. I guess I've met very few ladies, old or young who didn't like Ronnie Calloway. I hated with all of my heart to see him going through all of this again. Needless to say, we kept a smile on our faces and faith-filled words in our mouths. We kept in mind the Word of God which states that death and life are in the power of the tongue, and they who indulge in it shall eat the fruit of it for death or life. (Proverbs 18:20

AMP) We learned to speak life over our lives and you should be deliberate to do that also over your lives.

Ronnie developed a blood clot in his right leg, known as a DVT or a deep vein thrombosis. He had to take medication for that clot to dissolve. He was also on blood pressure medication and something else for the cancer. His oncologist encouraged Ronnie to get a full body scan which included injecting another chemical. Ronnie politely told the doctor that he would think about that.

Day after day Ronnie believed God for his healing. He studied the Bible every day. Our king size bed was covered with study books, different Bible versions, and commentaries as he fed himself the Word of God on healing. Christian television and healing videos played daily in our bedroom.

At night I cuddled up close behind Ronnie as he slept on his side. I desperately prayed for him. He had lost so much weight. I could literately feel his hip and shoulder bones protruding. I wept silently as my pillow became wet with my tears.

As time passed Ronnie's condition worsened. He had consented to taking those medications for a while. He also finally decided to get the PET scan defined as a Positron emission tomography.

He said to me, " Jack, I just want to see for myself how I'm doing." Sadly, the scan revealed clearly how he was doing. The cancer had metastasized to his bones and other organs. I was devastated. However, Ronnie maintained a positive attitude. He caressed my face in the palm of his hand and told me to smile. I did smile for him as the tears began to roll down my face. We both knew this was serious. We silently held one another tightly while I gathered my emotions. I'm crying again now as I recall and pen this account.

A week later Ronnie told me that he wasn't going to take all of this medicine anymore. He said he just didn't feel like himself. He wanted all of this out of his system. He assured me that was what he wanted.

We proceeded with our caregiving routine as Ronnie grew weaker and weaker. Much of my time with him was spent reading the Bible to him and talking about how much we loved each other.

As time passed, Ronnie could no longer walk. More nurses were brought on to help me care for him. God supernaturally supplied all of our need according to His riches in Glory by Christ Jesus.(Philippians 4:19 AMP) At one time Ronnie had six different nurses on different shifts on different days.

Because he could no longer move his legs, he would scoot around in our king size bed. That became dangerous because sometimes he would get too close to the edge and almost fall out. We finally and reluctantly called hospice mainly for the equipment they would provide. Ronnie was totally against having them until Stacy told him he could get better and graduate from hospice. That sounded like a challenge to Ronnie.

When they brought in the twin bed with the guard rails, Ronnie said with a loud voice "Whose gonna sleep in that? I'm not! That looks like a bed I slept in when I was a boy in the projects. I'm not sleeping in that bed!" We all thought that was so funny. Ronnie had to laugh at himself after he thought about it.

I said to him, "Dad, it is so important that you do not fall out of the bed and bleed out. We are doing all we can to protect you and help you heal. But you have to cooperate with us to help you."

He said, " Well, I'm not sleeping in that bed tonight, I'm sleeping with you tonight." Ronnie was so funny. He was getting tired of all the nurses and people in our house. He was very protective of the sanctity of our home. Our daughter Rhonda, and grandson Azlan were hired by the home health care company to help with his care and he liked that.

One day Stacy the head nurse called me. She said, "Hi Jackie, did you know that Ronnie fired all the nurses today?"

I said, "What?"

She said, "He told them thank you, but I don't need you to come back anymore. He said, Jack can take care of me now." They told Stacy he was very nice about it. I went upstairs immediately to Ronnie.

I asked calmly, "Dad, why did you fire the nurses today?"

He said, "Jack, I'm tired of all these people in our house. You're doing a great job and I just want to spend time with you."

I said, "Okay, I want to spend time with you too baby, but I need those nurses. It's a load off of my mind to know you are getting quality care Babe. I'm overseeing everything but I need those nurses."

He pulled me close and said, "Okay baby, I'm sorry. I just have so much to talk to you about."

I said, "Dad, I'll make sure no one is here at night or on the weekends. But love, you know you can talk to me anytime day or night." We kissed and I got Stacy back on the phone quickly. Please send the nurses back. She laughed and sent the nurses back.

CHAPTER 19

SACRED MOMENTS PRODUCE PRECIOUS MEMORIES

Another month passed and Ronnie still believed God for his healing. However, he also decided, going to heaven wasn't a bad idea either. There is a Scripture in the Message Translation of the Bible which states:

> She was forgiven many, many sins, and so she is very, very grateful. If forgiveness is minimal, the gratitude is minimal.
>
> (Luke 7:47)

Therefore, I tell you, her sins, many (as they
are), are forgiven her because she has loved
much. But he who is forgiven little loves little. (Luke 7:47 AMP)

Ronnie Calloway had been forgiven much as we all
have. He just chose to love Jesus and people much more
than so many of us do. He was more than grateful to God
for forgiving him of his sins. He was grateful to God for
giving him another opportunity to be all that God had
called him to be. God gave him another chance to be the
husband and father and grandfather God wanted him to
become. He was always quick to praise God in word and
deed. He also said to me often, "I thank God for you Jack."

When Ronnie surmised that he might not live much
longer on this earth, he began to prepare for heaven. He
got our house in order spiritually, financially and practi-
cally.

Ronnie asked me, " Jack, what would you do if I leave
and go to heaven?"

I answered quickly, "I'd do what I've always done Babe,
I would trust the Lord with all of my heart. But I would
miss you like crazy boyfriend."

He said, "You're so sweet. But seriously Jack, do you
think I have fulfilled my God-given purpose?"

I responded, "Oh, my goodness, I believe you absolutely have fulfilled your purpose. First of all, you yielded your life to Jesus Christ and made him the Lord of your life. You repented of everything you think you've done wrong. Then you reconciled with me and your daughters. You've made me the happiest and most loved woman on earth in my opinion. You've also lived a man of God life before us and the world. Not to mention all of the couples, and men specifically, you have counseled, mentored and ministered to. Dad, I believe you have definitely fulfilled your purpose."

He smiled and replied, "Well, I'm not finished yet."

From that day on many friends, family and acquaintances called to see how he was doing. Ronnie took those opportunities to minister to them.

He'd say to them before the call ended, "Are you saved? Do you know Jesus Christ? I don't want to miss you in heaven."

Then he started calling people to come to see him. He summoned them to his bedside. Ronnie gave people his final suggestions and instructions for their lives. It was inspiring for me to watch. Those were also exciting times for him. He loved giving instructions.

Our friends Ray and Polly came often and brought Ronnie soup and the Word. Ray and Ronnie grew up together in the projects. Ronnie had many lifelong friends. Pastor Frierson also came often to pray for Ronnie. He was one of Ronnie's many golf students.

Aside from all of the other people, Ronnie wanted to talk to me. We talked day and night. I sat with him as we reminisced about our fifty-two years together. We went back to when we met in 1965. We talked about how he swept me off my feet and talked about how we married one month later. We never recommended that to anyone. He said, "You couldn't resist me could you?" We laughed about how country I was, when I first came to Denver from Huntington, West Virginia.

Ronnie said, "Jack I always loved you from day one. I just didn't know how to be a Godly husband at that time. I had never seen one. But I always loved you. Please forgive me for all of the hurt I caused you in that old marriage. I was so selfish and so full of lust."

"Ronnie, you know I forgave you in 1996 when I married you again. Baby all of that is buried. I've always loved you too Ronnie Calloway. You have made me the happiest woman alive. Your tender touch, your sweet, sweet kisses always make my day. You have proven to me what marriage God's way looks and feels like."

Ronnie said, "Remember Jack when we would go to the Shapes and the Baja night clubs and dance. You were just 19 and had the longest prettiest legs I had ever seen."

"Yes boy, you were full of lust." We laughed and talked for hours even remembering when the girls were born.

We said, "Remember when Rhonda was a baby and you used to iron her diapers? They wouldn't hold water. When Chaunci was born and you were in the delivery room running around like a wild man?" We laughed and talked for hours for the last three weeks of Ronnie's life here on earth.

Ronnie, think about all of the old broke- down cars we have had over the years. You've come a long way baby. We tried to recall everything we needed to ask each other. He told me all about the bank accounts. He made sure he didn't leave me with any bills to pay.

Husbands, that would be a wonderful goal for you to work toward. God will help you do that if you ask and believe Him for it.

I believe God wants us believers in Christ Jesus, to know how to live on this earth and to know how to leave this earth. This is not our home; we're just passing through.

Ronnie said to me, "Jack, I'm ready to go home to be with the Lord. I'm not afraid to leave here. I have been reading about heaven for years and I'm excited to go. I'm tired of lying in this bed taking medicine and not able to move. God has promised me eternity in a new body and I'm ready."

"Ugh, I kinda don't know what to say Dad because this is a change of thinking for you."

"No, I've been thinking this way since the Pet scan, but I just haven't said it out loud. I knew then I might be headed home. You know, I only have one drawback. I don't want to leave you. I love you so much."

"I don't want you to leave me either Dad, but I hate to see you lying here suffering. Not able to go on the golf course and do the things you enjoy."

He interrupted me, "Jack, I'm not suffering!

I'm in some pain yes, but you all are taking real good care of me. I'm just ready to see Jesus."

After that conversation, his thoughts were geared toward heaven and taking as many people with him as possible.

Ronnie began a rapid decline. Nonetheless, he wanted to continue to talk to me about us daily. We remembered good times: the fun we had on all the cruises, the vacations we took with the girls. We laughed about taking three of our grandchildren on a cruise when they were little. Ronnie always interjected his love for me. I did the same for him. I told him what a good provider he had been for us. He told me what a great wife I had been for all the 52 years.

Ronnie wrote out the order of service he wanted for his memorial. He selected the people he wanted to perform specific tasks. He asked me if I could do his obituary.

I said, "Dad, I would be honored to do that for you."

He said, "Okay, I'll give you 15 minutes."

I laughed out loud and said, "15 minutes, what if I go over?"

He looked at me sternly and said, "You'll see!" We both laughed about that for a long time.

One day Ronnie said, "Jack, is there anything else we have forgotten to say? Can you think of anything else?"

I said, "No, but if I think of something I'll let you know brotha." Much of this was funny to us. We laughed at ourselves. That was such a strong characteristic of our marriage; we always laughed and played with each other even in the old marriage. We never wanted to get too serious even when dealing with death and dying. We saw the Scripture come to life: O death, where is your victory? O death, where is your sting?" For sin is the sting that results in death, and the law gives sin its power. But thank God! He gives us victory over sin and death through our Lord Jesus Christ. 1st Corinthians 15:55-58 (NLT)

As time progressed, Ronnie had to take a pill when he had severe pain, so he began to sleep a lot. One morning he woke up and looked at me and said, "Jack, am I still here?"

I said, "Yes love, and what do you want for breakfast?"

He laughed and said, "I thought for sure I left last night!"

I asked him, "Where did you go?"

He said, "To heaven of course!" We both laughed and kissed each other. We made Love without having sex those last few weeks.

Sadly, Ronnie took a severe turn for the worse. He ran a high fever and slept most of the time. Rhonda and Azlan had been out of town for a few days.

He awoke and asked, "Are the kids back yet?"

"No, not yet Babe, they'll be here soon." I replied.

They returned the next day.

Rhonda woke him up and said, "Dad, me and Azlan are home."

He opened his eyes, smiled really big and said, "Oh, my favorite visitors. I'm glad you're here baby."

The days passed and Ronnie awakened briefly off and on. He struggled to breathe sometime. The nurses put him on oxygen, but he kept taking it off. He *awaken* once and looked at me.

I whispered to him, "Ronnie I release you to go in Jesus' name." He looked at me and smiled and closed his eyes again.

The oxygen concentrator ran day and night. Then on December 6, 2020 Nurse Lynette was here with Ronnie all day. Nurse Stacy came later and stayed late. She rubbed Ronnie down with healing oil from head to toe. I remember her massaging his feet. His circulation was not good.

She said to him while he slept, "Ronnie Calloway you're all oiled up and you are going to just slide into heaven when you go."

She told me she didn't think it would be long. Ronnie's fever spiked that night after Stacy left. I was up most of the night putting cold cloths on his head and feet and praying. He was not waking or talking at all.

Rhonda had spent the night here at the house with me. When the fever finally broke I got into bed and tried to rest. Then at about 2 a. m. the Holy Spirit said to me, Pray in the Spirit and help usher Ronnie into heaven. I woke up Rhonda and told her let's pray in the Spirit over Dad. We began to pray in tongues over him. Finally, I had a release in my spirit. We ceased praying and went back to bed.

The next morning Lynette came at 7 a. m. She said she prayed that the oxygen concentrator would still be on. That would mean that Ronnie hadn't left during the night.

We were all being very attentive to Ronnie watching for any change.

I went in my bathroom and Lynette called out to me, "Jackie, come quickly." I did and she said, "There's been a noted change in his breathing."

I held Ronnie's hand as she listened to his heart with the stethoscope. I stared intently into his face when he took a long breath and then a short one and then no more. Lynette said, his heart is beating faintly.

She said, "Now it's trying to find a beat and now it just fluttered away. He is gone to heaven."

At first I was just numb. I wasn't crying I was just numb. I thought, what a *sweet parting*. There was no sting for me. Of course, Rhonda was crying but not uncontrollably.

Lynette said, "I will call hospice and they will call the coroner. Do you want some time alone with him Jackie?"

I said, "Please, that would be good." When they all left the room I just sat holding that same hand I had held for 52 years. While gently stroking and looking into that kind face. That face I had loved with all of my heart. This person who had known me better than anyone else on this earth. I kept thinking what a *sweet parting*. There was no sting in Ronnie's death. It was a *sweet parting*.

All I could say was, "Dad I pray that heaven is all you expected it to be and more. I never knew anyone who was so excited to get there. Thank you for loving me and taking care of me the way you did. God's way. We had a good long run. It was the best."

On December 7, 2020 at approximately 9:50 a.m. Ronnie Calloway took flight to be with Jesus Christ in heaven.

> Therefore, we are always confident, knowing that, whilst we are at home in the body, we are absent from the Lord: (For we walk by faith, not by sight:) We are confident, I say, and willing rather to be absent from the body, and to be present with the Lord.
>
> (2 Corinthians 5:6-8 KJV)

I was okay. I wasn't crushed. I missed Ronnie tremendously. However, we had tried to prepare me for his leaving as best we could. Ronnie, me and the Holy Spirit. Hence, I was not devastated.

We couldn't have the memorial because it was still COVID. Most churches were shut down.

The community outpouring, however, from friends, family and the church community was outstanding. People who knew us from radio and counseling showered us with spiritual and financial support and food. I was blessed and surprised at the response. People from all over the country reached out to me expressing their deepest sympathy. I heard from several of the golf courses' personnel across the city. They sent flowers, fruit and beautiful comments about Ronnie. He would have loved all the accolades. God is so good.

CHAPTER 20

*G*RIEVING WITH HOPE

I am not going to make this a long chapter. Nonetheless, since this book is designed to be an instruction manual for married couples to experience a glimpse of life in a marriage God's way, the Lord also wanted me to share briefly a little about death and grieving God's way.

Yes, it was truly a process for me. I learned when you love deeply you grieve even more deeply. When you love much you grieve much. When the two become one flesh you have much to grieve.

Therefore, shall a man leave his father and his mother, and shall cleave unto his wife; and they shall be one flesh.

(Genesis 2:24 KJV)

We truly became one flesh.

It's not just the physical person I grieved but all that came with that person. All the wonderful attributes Ronnie Calloway brought to me in our marriage I grieved.

Ronnie physically touching me.

His never-ending affection for me.

Him telling me he loved me every day.

Him cleaning the house.

Cooking meals for me.

Cutting the grass.

Never letting me lift anything over 5 lbs.

Always putting gas in the car.

Whistling at me so loudly no matter where we were.

Always holding my hand, kissing and caressing me in public.

Late at night laying his head in my lap as we watched television.

Telling me he needs a hug. Then squeezing me tightly for at least three minutes. Then ending that hug with a kiss.

Paying all the bills on time without me having to think about them.

Promoting and selling my book.

Supporting me in everything I did or wanted to do.

Being the greatest father ever.

These are all the things I had to grieve. I was fine until after Ronnie's Memorial on February 3, 2021. The next week I broke down and began to cry almost uncontrollably. I couldn't say Ronnie's name without crying. I told Rhonda I don't know if I'm crying this much or if tears are just pouring out of my eyes.

I kept quoting the Scripture that we don't grieve as those who have no hope. Correctly stated:

> Now also we would not have you ignorant, brethren, about those who fall asleep [[a]in death], that you may not grieve [for them] as the rest do who have no hope [beyond the grave]. (1 Thessalonians 4:13 AMP)

I not only know the Scriptures, but I know the God of all comfort who comforts me in all situations. I have an intimate relationship with Him, and have for years. That's what our lives, mine and Ronnie's, had been all about.

I knew without a doubt that Holy Spirit was going to heal me. The question was when? I became very ill in September of 2021. I had suspected pneumonia. I was sick for about two months. I was bedridden and under a doctor's care. They wanted to keep me in the hospital but Praise God for Lynette and Rhonda. I refused to stay in the hospital. There are two weeks that I don't remember at all. I didn't want to eat. My doctor suggested hospice. That was when I woke up to the realization of how sick I was.

I did think at one time, "Do I want to stay here or go be with Jesus and Ronnie?" It seemed that all of my fun had left the planet. The one who made me laugh was gone. I knew I would see him again, but when?

Finally, Holy Spirit said to me, "Why sit you here until you die?"

Needless to say, I got up.

Lynette got me a tricked out turquoise walker and I got up. I was on oxygen for months but I got up!

There were days I found myself on my hands and knees crying out to God. Asking Him to heal my heart. I told Him I didn't think I could physically continue to live if He didn't heal my heart. He encouraged me to continue to pray and stay in the Word. That was not difficult for me. I love the Word of God. I stayed in the word day and night. I believed what I read and I did what it said.

I continued to go to church most Sundays. I was told by my pastor that God is not finished with you yet. He said you will bear sweet fruit in your old age.

I gave myself a lot of grace to heal. I didn't let anyone push me to do anything I didn't want to do. Praise God I didn't have a job or small children to tend to. God and Ronnie had set me up well. I visited friends who have a place on the ocean. That helped me so much. I continued to cry but not as much. I missed Ronnie desperately.

I went to see a counselor one time which was very good for me. I was determined to heal. He suggested I sign up for this program titled Grief Share.org. It is held at a local church in the Denver area. This program was just what I needed. A thirteen-week class that convened once a week. It helped me to heal in a supernatural way. It is spiritually based. I went through the program three times. I recommend this national program to everyone I meet.

One morning while reading my Bible in my prayer room, I put the Bible down. I was prompted to pray in the Spirit. I continued to pray for about five or ten minutes. I stopped praying and sat quietly for a moment. Suddenly it was as if someone had taken a squeegee and swiped from inside of the top of my head all the way down my body to the tips of my toes on the inside. It seemed as if all the grief and sorrow was cleared out of my head, my heart and the rest of my body. It is difficult to explain but God healed me.

I stood up and felt so light healed from the top of my head to the soles of my feet. I began to praise God and I haven't stopped.

All of that heaviness and sorrow has been cleansed. It happened in January of 2024. I will forever love and miss Ronnie Calloway with all of my heart. However, I'm healed. The Scripture says:

> Surely he hath borne our griefs, and carried our sorrows: yet we did esteem him stricken, smitten of God, and afflicted. But he was wounded for our transgressions, he was bruised for our iniquities: the chastisement of our peace was upon him; and with his stripes we are healed. (Isaiah 53:4-5 KJV)

Moreover, the Lord brought to my attention that Ronnie and I *fulfilled* our marriage covenant. We vowed to love and to cherish for better for worse, in sickness and in health till death do us part. By the Grace of God, we did that.

I encourage all of you married couples to go back and read your wedding vows. Or maybe your pastor has the standard wedding vows you could read. I urge you to commit to God first, and to one another to fulfill your wedding vows. You can do this by the grace of God. It is a God requirement and the world is watching.

He who heeds instruction *and* correction is [not only himself] in the way of life [but also] is a way of life for others. And he who neglects *or* refuses reproof [not only himself] goes astray [but also] causes to err *and* is a path toward ruin for others.

(Proverbs 10:17 AMP)

I will leave you with this last reminder:

Therefore, if any person is (ingrafted) in Christ (the Messiah) he is a new creation (a new creature altogether); the old (previous moral and spiritual condition) has passed away. Behold, the fresh and new has come! But all things are from God, Who through Jesus Christ *reconciled* us to Himself (received us into favor, brought us into harmony with Himself) and gave to us the ministry of *reconciliation* (that by word and deed we might aim to bring others into harmony with Him). It was God (personally present) in Christ, *reconciling* and restoring the world to favor with Himself, not counting up and holding against (men) their trespasses (but canceling them), and committing to us the message of *reconciliation* (of restoration to favor). So, we are Christ's ambassadors, God making His appeal as it were through us. We (as Christ's personal representatives) beg you for His sake to lay hold of the divine favor (now offered you) and be *reconciled* to God. For our sake He made Christ (virtually) to be sin, so that in and through Him we might become (endued with, viewed as being in, and examples of) the righteousness of God (what we ought to be, approved and acceptable and in

right relationship with Him, by His goodness). (2nd Corinthians 5:17-21 AMP)

Love honor and cherish your spouse TILL DEATH DO
YOU PART.

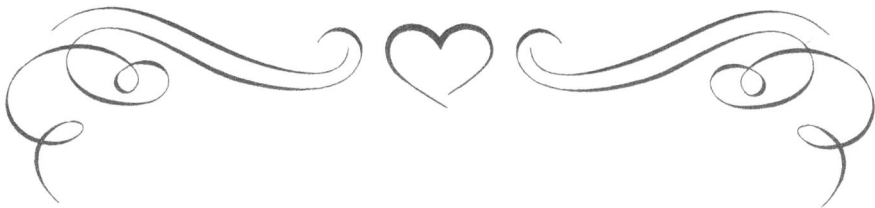

END NOTES

*Love That Would Not Let Me Go
By Jackie Calloway

Jackie Calloway had every reason not to love again. Her marriage was characterized by infidelity, grief, one disappointment after another, and divorce. But through God, she found strength not only to go on, but to believe in what seemed to be the impossible. That is just what her faithful God delivered.

**Suicide...Don't Do It
By Jackie Calloway

As a pregnant teen, fear drove Jackie to the brink of suicide. Now she shares her story with honesty and humility. She is hopeful that despite your situation, you will say "No" to death and "Yes" to life. Read how she defeated those suicidal thoughts, postpartum depression and continued to live. God always has a better way.

ABOUT THE AUTHOR

Jackie Calloway is an ordained minister, marriage counselor, reporter, television producer, and radio and television personality. She and her husband, Ronnie are founders of the Repairer of the Breach Ministries Inc. They counseled and helped countless couples reconcile through Christ. They also hosted a

radio broadcast bearing the same name. Jackie resides in Denver, Colorado and has three children, five grandchildren and three great grandchildren.

Connect with Me
Jackie Calloway
P.O. Box 473368
Aurora, Colorado 80047
rjcalloway@gmail.com
YouTube channel: healingfromcrisis